Anchored in the Current

Anchored in the Current

Discovering Howard Thurman
as Educator, Activist, Guide, and Prophet

Edited by Gregory C. Ellison II

WESTMINSTER
JOHN KNOX PRESS
LOUISVILLE • KENTUCKY

First edition
Published by Westminster John Knox Press
Louisville, Kentucky

20 21 22 23 24 25 26 27 28 29—10 9 8 7 6 5 4 3 2 1

Unless otherwise indicated, Scripture quotations are from the New Revised Standard Version of the Bible, copyright © 1989 by the Division of Christian Education of the National Council of the Churches of Christ in the U.S.A., and are used by permission. Scripture quotations marked ESV are from *The Holy Bible, English Standard Version,* © 2001 by Crossway Bibles, a publishing ministry of Good News Publishers. Used by permission. All rights reserved. Scripture quotations marked NIV are from *The Holy Bible, New International Version.* Copyright © 1973, 1978, 1984, 2011 by Biblica, Inc.® Used by permission. All rights reserved worldwide.

"Our Life and Times" poem, by Mari Evans, is reprinted by permission of the author. All rights reserved. Excerpts from Howard Thurman's *Disciplines of the Spirit, The Inward Journey,* and *The Growing Edge* are used by permission of Friends United Press. All rights reserved. Excerpts from *Jesus and the Disinherited* and *Meditations of the Heart,* by Howard Thurman, and *Lanterns: A Memoir of Mentors,* by Marian Wright Edelman, are reprinted by permission of Beacon. All rights reserved. Used by permission. Excerpt from Elesa Commerse, "The Lightning Rod of Loss and How It Compels Us to Be Kind," *Yoga Chicago* (March/April 2020), is used by permission of the author. All rights reserved.

Book design by Drew Stevens
Cover design by designpointinc.com
Cover photo by Joshua Earle on Unsplash

Library of Congress Cataloging-in-Publication Data is on file
at the Library of Congress, Washington, DC.

ISBN: 9780664260668

Contents

Contributors

Patrick D. Clayborn is the senior pastor of Bethel African Methodist Episcopal Church in Baltimore, Maryland. He is married to Rev. Sheri Smith Clayborn and has two children: Patrick II and Joya.

Elesa Commerse is the founder and codirector of Touching Earth Mindfulness Learning Center. She teaches meditation and mindful communication worldwide and offers intensive thematic studies and retreats for students committed to the practice.

Martin Doblmeier is the founder of Journey Films. He has produced more than thirty award-winning documentary films on topics of religion, faith, and spirituality, including *Bonhoeffer, The Power of Forgiveness,* and *Backs against the Wall: The Howard Thurman Story.*

Marian Wright Edelman, founder and president emerita of the Children's Defense Fund (CDF), has been an advocate for disadvantaged Americans for her entire professional life. For her life of service in the legal community and her advocacy on behalf of children, she received the Presidential Medal of Freedom, the nation's highest civilian award, in 2000.

Gregory C. Ellison II is Associate Professor of Pastoral Care and Counseling at Emory University's Candler School of Theology and founder of Fearless Dialogues. He is married to Antoinette and the proud father of Gregory III and Anaya.

Mari Evans was a poet, writer, playwright, and composer, associated with the Black Arts Movement. Instructed by her beloved teacher Langston Hughes, Evans's iconic poems like "I Am a Black Woman" and "Celebration" have been copiously cited and live on in the hearts of many.

Walter Earl Fluker is Martin Luther King, Jr. Professor of Ethical Leadership at Boston University School of Theology and editor and director of the Howard Thurman Papers Project.

Stephen Lewis is the president of the Forum for Theological Exploration (FTE) and creator of DO GOOD X, a start-up accelerator for diverse Christian social entrepreneurs. He is passionate about inspiring the next generation of leaders to make a difference in the world through Christian communities and businesses that do good in the world.

Parker J. Palmer is an independent writer, teacher, and activist. He holds a PhD from the University of California, Berkeley, and his ten books (most recently, *On the Brink of Everything: Grace, Gravity and Getting Old*) have been recognized with thirteen honorary doctorates.

Luke A. Powery is the dean of the Duke University Chapel and Associate Professor of Homiletics at Duke Divinity School. His most recent book is *Were You There? Lenten Reflections on the Spirituals*, and he also serves as a general editor for the nine-volume lectionary commentary series titled Connections: A Lectionary Commentary for Preaching and Worship.

Liza J. Rankow is an interfaith minister, activist, educator, and the founder of OneLife Institute for Spirituality & Social Transformation. She has taught classes on Thurman in community and academic settings since 2002 and is the producer and coeditor of a six-CD archival audio collection titled *The Living Wisdom of Howard Thurman* (Sounds True, 2010).

Tyler Ho-Yin Sit is a United Methodist pastor and church planter of New City Church in Minneapolis. He is author of the upcoming book tentatively titled *Staying Awake: The Gospel for Changemakers,* an exploration of Christianity from queer perspectives of color. @TylerSit

Luther E. Smith Jr. is Professor Emeritus of Church and Community, Candler School of Theology, Emory University. He is the author of *Howard Thurman: The Mystic as Prophet*, editor of *Howard Thurman: Essential Writings*, senior advisory editor for the "Howard Thurman Papers Project," coeditor of the recordings *The Living Wisdom of Howard Thurman: A Visionary for Our Time,* and author of numerous articles on Howard Thurman.

Shively T. J. Smith is Assistant Professor of New Testament at Boston School of Theology and an itinerant elder in the African Methodist Episcopal Church. Smith's scholarship focuses on the general letters, diaspora rhetoric, and hermeneutics.

Barbara Brown Taylor is a *New York Times* best-selling author, speaker, and Episcopal priest who taught at Piedmont College for twenty years, retiring as the Butman Professor Emerita of Religion in 2017.

Matthew Wesley Williams serves as the president at the Interdenominational Theological Center (ITC), a historically Black ecumenical graduate theological school, located in the heart of Atlanta, Georgia. He is coauthor of *Another Way: Living and Leading Change on Purpose* and resides in the Atlanta metropolitan area with his wife, Alexis, and children, Zuri and Sage.

Starsky D. Wilson is president and chief executive officer of Deaconess Foundation, a philanthropic child advocacy ministry in St. Louis, Missouri. He is board chair for the National Committee for Responsive Philanthropy and formerly led the Ferguson Commission.

Acknowledgments
A Letter to My Daughter on the
One Hundred Fifty-Seventh Anniversary
of the Emancipation

01 January 2020
Atlanta, Georgia

Dear Anaya:

My soul looks back and remembers April 2, 2009. Midnight rain glistened on Atlanta's cityscape as I raced down Interstate 85. While I dodged puddles at breakneck speed, I could not circumnavigate the water that just splashed on the passenger-seat floor. Your mother's voice rose over a guttural moan, "Her head is coming out . . . pull over!" As I steered the sedan to the right shoulder, the spinning tires hit divots in the concrete and mimicked the steady thump of our heartbeats. Time slowed to a steady crawl. After unsuccessfully flagging down a late-night commuter, I opened the passenger-side car door, and kneeled at your mother's side. Under the glimmer of the dim console lighting, your mother pushed. Time froze on that highway shoulder; even your two-year-old brother sensed from his front-facing car seat that a miracle was underway. Past, present, and future collapsed into a single Kairos moment, you burst into our lives, and we lifted a prayer of thanksgiving.

Unbound by chronological time, the ancient Greek word *Kairos* means an opportune moment for critical decision or decisive action. Such instances rupture the monotony of daily routine and have the potential to forever shape the character of a life. The dramatic unfolding of your birth has since alerted me to remain vigilantly aware of Kairos moments that might forever shift my trajectory. Two such providential incidents transpired to make this book you now hold a reality.

It was 2014 . . . Lofted by the bitter spring wind, snow flurries whirled midair before they instantly evaporated on the Nashville grass.

Warm-blooded at my core, I rushed into the crowded breakfast restaurant to be greeted by a broad-smiling gentle giant named Bob Ratcliff. Never before had we met, yet we laughed heartily as we exchanged pleasantries about our families. Only minutes after my pancakes arrived, Bob invited me to join the Westminster John Knox family and write two books with the Press—one on Fearless Dialogues and the other about Howard Thurman. Once again, the second hand slowed. I knew with a certain suddenness that this man and the Press's offer would alter my course. Kairos. Six years ago, I did not fathom that Bob Ratcliff would be far more than an editor. To my delight, he has been an advocate, voice coach, grief counselor, spiritual guide, and friend. For his generosity and kindness I give thanks.

During that pancake breakfast, I shared with Bob a dream of bringing together a host of luminaries whose vocations have been variously informed by the life, work, and witness of Thurman. Far more than a paper conference to discuss the components of an edited volume, I envisioned a gathering where those inspired by Thurman's legacy could breathe deeply, eat communally, and share stories of hope and freedom to strengthen us for the journey ahead. In September 2016, this dream came to be. On the celestial grounds of Alex Haley's Farm in Clinton, Tennessee, nearly twenty luminaries gathered to build beloved community and lay the foundation for this volume. On the Farm, the grass looked greener, the air tasted sweeter, the conversations lingered longer, and the sun seemed to stand still in the sky. On that September weekend I glimpsed heaven, and I am so grateful that for the rest of my days those memories will live in my head and heart.

You see, Anaya, Kairos moments stimulate gratitude. In that spirit I give thanks for the community of institutions that banded together so you and countless others could hold this book. I am deeply appreciative of the president, editorial staff, and marketing team of Westminster John Knox Press for their graciousness and care. Likewise, I am indebted to the Children's Defense Fund for their hospitality to the luminaries on the Farm and for providing the platform to launch this book in summer 2020. I especially commend the Louisville Institute and my colleagues at Candler School of Theology for their financial support of the 2016 gathering.

Each of the named contributors in this text and their loved ones occupy a special place in my heart as part of our family. I pray that in your lifetime you will meet and embrace: Patrick D. Clayborn, Elesa Commerse, Martin Doblmeier, Marian Wright Edelman, Mari

Evans, Walter Earl Fluker, Stephen Lewis, Luke A. Powery, Parker J. Palmer, Liza J. Rankow, Tyler Ho-Yin Sit, Luther E. Smith Jr., Shively T. J. Smith, Barbara Brown Taylor, Matthew Wesley Williams, and Starsky D. Wilson. A host of others have been central to the completion of this publication, including but not limited to: Blanches de Paula, Antoinette Ellison, Darren Ellison, Jeannette Ellison, Nikia Ellison, Adrian Epps, Sharon Watson Fluker, Clinton Greenaway, Jason Greenaway, LaVerne Greenaway, Nikki Greenaway, Shannon Daley Harris, C. Douglas Hollis Jr., Kai Jackson Issa, Angela Johnson, Jasmine "Jazzy" Johnson, Noble Jones, James Bernard Kynes Sr., Georgette "Jojo" Ledgister, Jill Lum, Iyabo Onipede, Jasmine Martin, Jasmine McGowan, Gideon Msazurwa, Rahiel Msazurwa, Julian Reid, Don Richter, Toby Sanders, Helen Pearson Smith, Tavares Stephens, Calvin Taylor, Ed Taylor, Gregory Vaughn, Sam White, Janet Wolf, and Floyd Wood. Lastly, I give thanks to our bloodline—those who stand shoulder-to-shoulder with us, and the ones, like your grandfather, who walk with the ancestors.

Know this, Anaya, it is no mistake that your mother and I chose "Kaira" as your middle name. Your very being is a daily reminder of the critical decisions and decisive actions precipitated through Kairos moments that alter our path. I implore you to walk in the boldness of your name, be ever careful to give thanks, and ensure that your brother does the same.

May the peace of the Eternal guide your every step.

Your father,

Greg

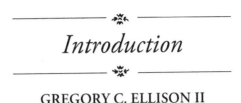

Introduction

GREGORY C. ELLISON II

There I stand above the fray, behind the sacred desk. Silently, I look on the unsettled sea as the roaring riptide of grief washes over the three thousand seated before me. Their eyes well with salted water; a torrential downpour on the face of my mourning mother. In arm's reach of the weeping widow bobs a wind-tossed wooden box. A frail craft, indeed, for transport to the great beyond. Yet, this casket carries the frame of a soul I know all too well. It is my father, my namesake, whom I must eulogize.

With the Spirit in me and the cloud of ancestral witnesses about me, I part my lips and from my core I speak: "Life was so much simpler then, that is, before the fifth day of the third month in the year of our Lord 2018. Then half past the eleventh hour of that day his fingers ran cold."

For the next thirty minutes, I move from the outer banks and carry with me three thousand into the deep. On the great waters of grief, we laugh, cry, remember, and internalize the challenge of a life moored to freedom. As the eulogy nears its close, I step from behind the sacred desk, descend the pulpit, and sit in a chair facing my mourning mother. I extend a hand. She draws me in.

Eye-to-eye and hand-to-hand with the one who birthed me, the shadow of the altar falls upon our shoulders. Cascading through the window to our left, refractions of magenta dance above our heads. Even

1

though thousands surrounded us in cushioned pews, in that moment it felt as if we sat alone, together—on an island with an altar guarded by an angel on the inward sea.[1] From that isle, the ground of my center began to quake and an ancestral voice, deep in register and marked by long pauses, emerged. The voice was not my own and neither was the question I would pose to my mother and the thousands drifting on the unsettled sea: "What must I do to die a good death?"

Silence hung heavy in the air like nimbus clouds waiting to wail. From that island, I speak once more, "This inquiry was first asked by Howard Washington Thurman, who believed that life and death are of a single respiration. To this end, one might only achieve a good death by living a good life." Then, an atmospheric change. The thick air of silence dissipates. The clouds break. A gentle calm passes over the sea, as I reflect on how the last minutes of my father's time on Earth were indicative of a good death and a testament to a life well lived.

On the most tumultuous week of my forty-two-year-old life, I was tasked with comforting a community and offering solace to my family. Beleaguered, I struggled to find my own sea legs in the surging current of grief. Howard Thurman was my ANCHOR.

IN SEARCH OF AN ANCHOR

Anchors provide stability; they ground us, solidifying our sometimes-insubstantial confidence. Facing the grim reality of my namesake's sudden unexpected death, I hardly anticipated a gentle calm. Yet, hours before my father's eulogy, I sat in the sanctuary of Luther Smith's basement library. Books gifted by Howard Thurman surrounded me. Thumbing through Thurman's *For the Inward Journey,* a familiar meditation titled "The Good Death" straightened my spine. As I walked through the words on the page, Thurman's question on mortality and legacy offered steady footing: words that could challenge and comfort, offer stability and security for the uncertain days ahead. Five years before that moment, in a season of vocational crisis, I found myself wedged in by the limiting labels of professor, minister, and activist. Thurman's interpretations of a boundary-breaking poor Jewish man in *Jesus and the Disinherited* led me out of that corner. More than a decade ago, under the intensified pressures of applying for a tenure-track professor's position at Emory University, I chanted Thurman's "How Good to Center Down" to find peace as "the streets of my mind seethed with endless traffic."[2] In short, Thurman's wisdom offered an anchoring assurance in the highest and lowest of days.

If you have picked up this book, you too may be in search of an anchor. Might Thurman offer a source of abiding confidence for you? Perhaps you know of Howard Thurman as one who mentored Dr. Martin Luther King Jr. or even as the one who swapped theories of nonviolence with Gandhi. Maybe you have thumbed through one of his twenty-three books or you have leaned in close to feel the vibrations of his baritone voice on a recorded sermon. It is possible that you were drawn to Thurman by reference to his famed address "The Sound of the Genuine" or his oft-quoted words, "Don't ask what the world needs. Ask yourself what makes you come alive, and go do that. . . ." Or, you may know nothing of Thurman, and you picked up this book because of its poetic title, its captivating cover, or one of the dynamic authors in this text. Regardless of how you have come, beloved reader, we welcome you.

Brace yourself. The following sentence may surprise you. This book is not *just about* Howard Thurman. Certainly, in this introduction I will offer a brief biographical overview. But, *Anchored in the Current* illumines how the life, work, and wisdom of Howard Thurman has served as an anchor for me and the sixteen accomplished educators, ministers, artists, and activists who have contributed writings in this text.

The authors in this text were carefully selected to guide you on this journey. They, too, have served as anchors, as wise teachers, as kinfolk to me. Each was chosen because of their creative usage of Thurman's wisdom in their work and their ability as writers to capture the imagination while conveying facts. Also know that, like Thurman, each moves nimbly on the edges of vocational labels where categories like minister, educator, institution builder, artist, or activist function as mere placeholders. Finally, those gathered on these pages represent a multitude of diversities (e.g., race, culture, generation, sexual identity, faith background). Together, we reflect an extension of Thurman's lifelong quest for beloved community. Without further ado, I am honored to introduce you to your shipmates, your guides, my family.

In step with Thurman's solidarity with the disinherited, Presidential Medal of Freedom awardee Marian Wright Edelman has devoted her life to advocating for children and disenfranchised Americans. Best-selling authors Barbara Brown Taylor and Parker J. Palmer have demonstrated in their writing a commitment to issues of education, vocation, and the spiritual life that align with Thurman's corpus of published works. The late, great poet Mari Evans dedicated her life to penning pieces that invite readers into creative encounters that awaken the mind and stir the soul. I am honored that prior to her passing, Ms. Mari wrote a poem especially for this book. Both Luther Smith and Walter Fluker were mentees of Thurman and have focused much of their scholarship on sharing their teacher's wisdom with the world. In the spirit of Thurman's open-minded probing, New Testament scholar Shively Smith never shies away from posing penetrating questions of sacred texts. Luke Powery, Dean of the Chapel at Duke University, employs Thurman in his preaching, as does Patrick Clayborn, pastor of Bethel AME Church, a thriving congregation in Baltimore, Maryland. As pioneering institution builders, Elesa Commerse, Stephen Lewis, and Matthew Wesley Williams draw on Thurman's legacy of creating spaces for the spirit to guide complex decision making. Possessing an uncanny ability to communicate across generational boundaries, award-winning documentarian Martin Doblmeier has taken the stories of religious icons like Thurman to the big screen. Whether standing on the frontlines of a protest, preaching prophetically from a pulpit, or strategizing over policy in a boardroom, Starsky D. Wilson embodies Thurman's ideal of fusing spirituality and social action. Tyler Ho-Yin Sit, Liza Rankow, and I have employed the life and work of Thurman as a model for prophetic service and community engagement. I trust that each of these guides will function as a compass as you chart the inward sea.

A last word on anchors. Given Thurman's wide-reaching influence and the manifold experiences of the selected authors, *Anchored in the Current* is divided into four sections: Thurman as Vocational Anchor, Thurman as Anchor for Educators, Thurman as Anchor for Activists, and Thurman as Spiritual Anchor. For coherence and continuity, a quote or passage from Thurman's work begins most chapters. Through powerful personal narratives, historical snapshots, and interpretive insights, each author illumines how the chosen quote or passage informs their life, work, and daily practice. It must not be overlooked, beloved reader, that each chapter concludes with grounding questions. More on the importance of these questions later. Finally, to offer buoyancy to these weighty issues of the spirit, a brief meditative interlude introduces each of the four sections.

As promised, I conclude this introduction with a brief biographical overview of Howard Thurman's life. To provide a foretaste of the chapters, in short measure, I chronicle the life of Thurman as vocational guide, educator, activist, and spiritual pioneer. However, I am the grandson of a griot, and like my grandpa, Willie "Dub" Simpson, storytelling sinews my body, mind, and spirit. So, in step with the contributing authors, I offer four brief narratives of how Thurman has inspirited my life in each of these areas. Consistent with the chapters to follow, I end with an invitation to question, "Why drop anchor in the current?"

Grab your life preserver. Come with me now. There's work for us far beyond the harbor bar.

THURMAN AS VOCATIONAL ANCHOR

Born forty-four days before the turn of the twentieth century, Howard Washington Thurman was raised in the segregated town of Daytona Beach, Florida. Reared by a widowed mother with few financial means, from an outsider's view upward mobility for the young Thurman seemed bleak. But his grandmother, Nancy Ambrose, who was born a slave, "did not allow him to accept the educational limitations placed on black youth in their community."[3] Spurred by a need to assist his family, a hope from ages past, and a commitment to personal growth, Thurman became the first African American youth in Daytona Beach to receive an eighth-grade certificate from the public schools—all while working full-time at a fish market.[4] His certificate and 99-percent grammar school grade point average in hand, Thurman's quest for knowledge remained unquenched.[5]

Back in the early 1900s, only three public high schools existed for African American youth in Florida. With the little money he had saved, Thurman applied and was accepted to the Florida Baptist Academy of Jacksonville. During these high school years, Thurman solicited the wisdom of two pioneering African American educators, Mary McLeod Bethune and Mordecai Wyatt Johnson. In arm's reach of the Daytona-based Bethune, Thurman sought counsel from the founder of Bethune-Cookman College. Yet, Thurman had never met Johnson in person; he only admired him from afar.

In his final year of high school, Thurman felt the pressing need of additional vocational guidance, so he wrote a letter of introduction to Johnson. "Listen while I tell to you my soul," the young Thurman opens. In the first paragraphs, Thurman details his high school hardships and academic accomplishments. He shares that though he had insufficient winter garments, worked long shifts, and only ate one square meal per day, he finished his first year with a 96-percent grade point average, the highest in the school. In his second and third year of high school, he earned a 98 percent and 94 percent respectively.[6] After briefly chronicling his academic transcript, Thurman bares his soul more deeply by outlining a vocational vision few teenagers could ever articulate:

> I want to be a minister of the Gospel. I feel the needs of my people. I see their distressing conditions, and have offered myself upon the altar as a living sacrifice, in order that I may help the "skinned and flung down" . . . . I am scheduled to finish here next year. As you know the war is on and young men are being snatched daily. I am patriotic, I am willing to fight for democracy, but my friend Rev. Johnson, my people need me. . . .[7]

In search of a vocational anchor—one who might help him integrate his love of learning, his spiritual longing, and his commitment to liberation—the eighteen-year-old Thurman concludes his letter to Johnson with a prayer request: "Please pray for me because {almost} on every hand, I am discouraged in my choice of the Ministry. Sometimes I think nobody cares but thank God, Jesus does, mother does, and I believe you do."[8]

In this letter—the earliest surviving correspondence in Thurman's voluminous papers—we hear an adolescent longing for companionship, affirmation, and guidance. You may know the lonesome feeling of possessing a dream that few around you understand. In your gut, you may feel the pit of striving without recognition or the despair of aimless meandering without a guide. Like young man Thurman, every apprentice yearns for a wise teacher. I, too, knew this longing.

It was no ordinary class. I put aside my lecture notes, and on that brisk fall afternoon in my second year of teaching, I sat in the circle of seminarians as they disclosed their truths. Fingers fidgeted. Breaths grew long. One gazed at the ceiling as silent tears fell. With each disclosure the room strangely warmed and the windows seemed to sweat as the tropic conditions in the classroom met the chilled air on the opposite side of the pane. An uneasy quiet hung in the air. I closed my eyes and behind the darkness of my eyelids, "I [saw] their distressing condition." "I [felt] the needs of my people." I parsed the silence with words, but those words were not my words; they felt ancient. From the darkness, I spoke of comfort, challenge, change.

Like the colored autumn leaves blowing beyond the glass, the ancestral words moved among us, changing us, healing us. Silent tears became audible weeping. Deep sighs morphed into guttural moans. The fidgeter now stood rocking. Back and forth she swayed. Amid the ancient words and swell of emotion, a fulsome energy rested on me like an anvil; wresting in me an immovable mass.

Overcome by the weighty energy of carrying the ancient words, I opened my eyes. Before me, a downpour of tears, thundering moans, and a woman swaying as if the ground beneath her quaked. Overwhelmed by such atmospheric shifts, I shut off the ancestral spigot of words mid-sentence. I stood. Rushed out the building. I did not return to class.

Neither the students nor I had ever quite experienced a moment like that. To further discern what occurred, I sought the counsel of a senior colleague who moved more like a monk than professor. He explained that in that classroom I had become "a healer of souls." The monkish professor advised, "You must now pray for teachers that will help you hone that gift."

In my prayers, I petitioned for teachers. Within eighteen months, four teachers—each one a healer of souls—entered my life. I stood in arm's reach of three of these teachers. One I admired from afar. To the latter, I sent a letter of introduction to tell my soul, share my academic pedigree, and seek guidance for my vocational quest. For nearly a decade, Mari Evans, Barbara Brown Taylor, Parker J. Palmer, and Luther Smith have been vocational anchors for me. I call them my "Council of Yodas," and I am their apprentice learning to use "God's force."

Evans, Taylor, and Palmer have uniquely carved out a living as writers who guide their audiences to see the Divine in the seemingly mundane. These three Yodas bare their souls in the first three entries of this book, and offer insights on how Thurman altered their vision of vocation. From their reflections, I hope that you might come to see your vocation anew and learn from them creative ways to use "God's force" for the generational good.

THURMAN AS ANCHOR FOR EDUCATORS

After graduating from Florida Baptist Academy as valedictorian, Thurman continued his schooling at Morehouse College. During his collegiate years, Thurman read every book in the library, served as class president, edited the school's literary magazine, and graduated once again as valedictorian.[9] Though mentors at Morehouse encouraged him to pursue further studies in economics, Thurman enrolled as one of two African Americans at Rochester Theological Seminary in fall of 1923. While in upstate New York, Thurman garnered acclaim as a "prominent educator" and thoughtful speaker on matters of race. In a biographical essay about Thurman's seminary years, Walter Earl Fluker exclaims, "Thurman conducted his speaking engagements amid Rochester's hostile racial climate that was further agitated by the presence of the Ku Klux Klan . . . [whose] members would regularly attend his speeches."[10] In spite of Thurman's full roster of speaking engagements and a "punishing study schedule that left him with little leisure time," in May 1926, Thurman graduated again as valedictorian.[11]

In the days following graduation, Thurman married Katie Kelly and undertook his first pastorate at Mount Zion Baptist Church in Oberlin, Ohio. Weeks after assuming his post as Mount Zion's pastor, Thurman enrolled in postgraduate studies at Oberlin Graduate School of Theology. From his base in Ohio, over the next two years, Thurman toured the country: lecturing, preaching, and testing theories he crafted in his years of schooling at Florida Baptist, Morehouse, Rochester, and Oberlin.[12] One must not overlook that the not-yet thirty-year-old African American Thurman received many of these invitations from predominantly white institutions who expected him to address volatile subjects such as faith, economics, and race. Given his experiences of fearlessly teaching before Klan members in Rochester, one might gather that Thurman stood unwaveringly as he delivered these tinderbox addresses in classrooms, conference halls, and church houses marked by race, class, and theological divides.

To my knowledge, I have never addressed Klan members in a teaching setting. However, during my doctoral student days, I received the good fortune of testing theories I learned at Douglass High, Emory, and Princeton Theological Seminary in an unconventional educational environment that many might see as a powder keg. To be sure, this was no ordinary classroom. Sans chalkboard, some sessions were held behind thick paned glass, bolted metal doors, and narrow barred windows. Need I mention, these were no ordinary pupils. Hardened by gunplay, fallen friends, and an unforgiving drug culture, these young Black and brown men sought vestiges of hope as they transitioned out of the criminal justice system and back into their communities. Under the guard's gaze, I was slated to be their teacher. Or so I thought.

Shielded beneath their urban exoskeleton lay compassionate hearts, untapped artistic gifts, and lofty vocational aspirations. Yet, these qualities often remained unnurtured because these students could not figure out how to escape punitive perceptions and life-limiting labels like "felon," "thug," or "dropout." Knowing full well their tensions of being wedged between the hypervisibility of stigmatizing stereotypes and the invisibility of shielded dreams, on one afternoon class, I introduced the young men to Howard Thurman's elegy to the unseen, "A Strange Freedom."

With one strong reader in every group, I invited them to recite each word in every sentence slowly and deliberately. A cacophony of baritoned words rose to the ceiling, and before crashing to the floor they fell upon fertile hearts. My eyes scanned the room. Some read slowly. Others closed their eyes, sculpting mental images from the picturesque soliloquy. Nearly ten minutes into the exercise, the once discordant voices took on the pitch, shape, and character of a meditative Gregorian chant. As the final voice trailed off into a contemplative quiet, the young men sat spellbound by Thurman's timeless truth.

Stepping into that solemn space, I encouraged the young men to identify the sentences or scenes in Thurman's meditation that most clearly defined their present reality. Group after group chose the same section:

> To be ignored, to be passed over as of no account and of no meaning, is to be made into a faceless thing, not a man [woman]. It is better to be the complete victim of an anger unrestrained and a wrath which knows no bounds, to be torn asunder without mercy or battered to a pulp by angry violence, than to be passed over as if one were not. Here at least one is dealt with, encountered, vanquished, or overwhelmed—but not ignored. It is a strange freedom to go nameless up and down the streets of other minds where no salutation greets and no sign is given to mark the place one calls one's own.[13]

Like Thurman, these young men knew all too well the felt reality of risking life and limb in order to be seen. Yet for them, facing death for the sake of street recognition offered little freedom to live. A few articulated the captivity of labels like felon, others mentioned the numbing pain of muteness and invisibility. I can still hear one young man saying, "No salutation greets a thug . . . just, thug shit greets a thug." To be known by one's name, not by one's reputation or criminal record, was to be more than a faceless thing.

Far from the tidied classrooms on Princeton's lush green campus, in

Newark's concrete jungle I shared Thurman's elegy on freedom with young men who felt physically and psychologically bound. The Gregorian chant of their voices, their will to understand, and the heartfelt discussion on Thurman's meditation uncovered three epiphanies that continue to guide my teaching: First, the quest to learn, know, and be known transcends differences like race, class, and literacy. Second, if properly framed, a seemingly destructive physical space can become an optimal learning environment. Third, timeless truths possess qualities that can capture the imagination of unlikely partners from college students and gang leaders to corporate executives and Klansmen.

In the second section of *Anchored in the Current*, Martin Doblmeier, Walter Earl Fluker, and Shively Smith invite you to consider how Thurman's teachings might alter how you interpret the world around you. Doblmeier, who creates documentaries to introduce the general public to religious pioneers, speaks of lessons he learned from Thurman's life while producing the Emmy Award–winning film, *Backs against the Wall: The Howard Thurman Story*. Fluker, an archivist of Thurman's papers, offers personal accounts of classroom sessions with Thurman and his teacher's lasting influence on his scholarship. Smith, who shared that reading Thurman during her international studies in Oxford lessened her homesickness, now draws upon Thurman's interpretive lens to read Scripture. Each in their own way, like me, has been anchored by Thurman as they teach and learn with diverse audiences.

THURMAN AS ANCHOR FOR ACTIVISTS

If you were to chart the history of the civil rights movement in America, you might be tempted to exclude Thurman from the list of activists committed to that struggle. Not so fast. Some of his compatriots would beg to differ. "Howard Thurman was a saint of the Movement," exclaimed Congressman John Lewis. "He helped to establish the philosophical framework of how to struggle. 'You cannot let the oppressor break your spirit. They can break your bones, your arms, but not your spirit,'" added Rev. Jesse Jackson. To these points, Rev. Otis Moss Jr. furthered, "[Thurman] gave us the basis for the march, [so] that we'd know why we marched, the principles upon which we marched, how we marched, and what we'd do after the march."[14] Yet, Thurman was no ordinary movement maker, for he viewed the spiritual worker as possessing a unique disposition that releases forces into the ecosystem to stimulate social change.

Thurman's theories of social change began percolating during his later years in Ohio. In a 1927 correspondence to Mordecai Wyatt Johnson, Thurman noted, "[One must] release to the full our greatest spiritual powers, that there may be such a grand swell of spiritual energy that existing systems will be upset from sheer dynamic."[15] Thurman further asserts that a new kind of education about Jesus is necessary to address this problem.

These reflections on Jesus would evolve more as he transitioned from his pastorate in Ohio to accept his first job in academia. In the fall of 1929, Thurman and his family returned to Atlanta, where he served as a lecturer in philosophy and religion at his alma mater, Morehouse, and its sister school, Spelman College. In a Spelman class titled "The Bible as Living Literature," Thurman tested ideas that would become the foundation of his interpretation of the boundary-breaking Jesus.[16] While he was inching closer to making vital connections in the classroom between the oppressive racial climate of the United States and Jesus' life as a poor Jew in the Roman world, his wife fell ill. Katie Kelly died on December 21, 1930. She was survived by her daughter, Olive, and her husband, Howard.

Though the shadow of Katie's death lingered near, Thurman maintained a grueling schedule of speaking engagements. Ridden with physical and emotional exhaustion, he willed himself to complete the academic year. At semester's end, the bereaved widower sought the solace of the sea. Knowing not a single soul in Europe, Thurman crossed the Atlantic for the first time. There, he spent the summer in London, Scotland, Paris, and Geneva reevaluating his personal and professional goals. Somewhere between the cobbled stone streets of London and the grassed uplands of Scotland, an epiphany shifted Thurman's gaze:

> I moved into profound focus; the direction of the future opened wide its doors. My life seemed whole again and the strains of the unknown melody healed my innermost center. . . . I was aware that God was not yet done with me, that I need never fear the darkness, nor delude myself that the contradictions of life are final. I was ready now for the journey.[17]

Beyond these words in his autobiography, little mention is made about the impact of Thurman's first international excursion on his future outlook. However, I surmise that the onset of suffering and deep reflections on mortality unleashed in Thurman a search for clarity on the intersections between spirituality and social action.

Just months after his return from Europe, Thurman gave a lecture in February 1932 to a packed auditorium in Atlanta titled "The Kind of Religion the Negro Needs in Times Like These." A brief published account of the talk stated that Thurman reflected on how "the religion espoused by the 'lowly Nazarene' had received much of its significance from the fact that its exponent was a member of a despised circumscribed minority group."[18] Thurman's fearless 1932 talk about the poor Jew who stood with the disenfranchised would be expanded into a more robust essay titled "Good News for the Underprivileged." That essay would provide the pillars of Thurman's most renowned book, *Jesus and the Disinherited*.

In that famed monograph, Thurman speaks of his second voyage across the Atlantic's raging seas in 1935. Joined by his second wife, Sue Bailey Thurman, and two others, Thurman, who was then teaching at Howard University, embarked on a "Pilgrimage of Friendship." The four-person Negro delegation left New York City for a four-month tour across India, where Thurman spoke at least 135 times in fifty different cities. After his first lecture in India, Thurman encountered a series of questions from a university administrator that shook him at his core and forced him to distill his ideas on spirituality and social action.

The administrator simply asked, "*What are you doing here?*" The Hindu host wondered aloud how Thurman could claim the same Christian tradition utilized to impose political segregation, social isolation, and economic inequality on his own people. After listing this diatribe of ills, the administrator crudely invited Thurman to conversation by calling him "a traitor to all the darker peoples of the earth."[19] That afternoon, Thurman and the Hindu administrator engaged in five hours of fearless dialogue about Thurman's commitment to the religion of Jesus.

Over a decade after the five-hour conversation, Thurman published *Jesus and the Disinherited*. A bold social application of Thurman's biblical interpretation, the book undermines religious justification for segregation, asserts the worth of the underprivileged, and confronts structures complicit with injustice.[20] In order to make the case that the underprivileged have direct access to God, Thurman located Jesus as one of the disinherited in his age. This interpretative lens provided a unique angle to examine Jesus' unconventional approach to contesting oppressive systems.

One other key encounter in India would forever frame Thurman's approach to spirituality and social action: his three-hour meeting with Mahatma Gandhi. In this brief exchange, Gandhi exacted a shrewd examination of American society through "persistent, pragmatic questions about American Negroes, the course of slavery, . . . voting rights, lynching, discrimination, public school education, the churches and how they functioned." Moments before the meeting's close, Thurman inquired of Gandhi's tactics for breaking the age-old caste system. In response, Gandhi posited, "I became the spearhead of a movement for the building of a new self-respect, a fresh self-image for the untouchables in Indian society. I felt that the impact of this would be *the release of energy* needed to sustain a commitment to nonviolent direct action."[21]

In short, Gandhi's approach to releasing a spiritual energy that reframed the mind and altered the perception of the most stigmatized mirrored Thurman's 1929 correspondence to Mordecai Wyatt Johnson. Both sought to release a grand swell of spiritual energy to collapse existing systems. By 1948, Thurman had refined his understanding of the mystic's role as a conduit of social change through channeling spiritual energy:

> [The mystic] is no coward, sticking his [her] head in the sand. Praying to God because he [she] is scared or because he [she] does not have the nerve to do anything else. But he [she] is sure that he [she] is in touch with terrible energy. And if his [her] life can be a point of focus through which that energy hits its mark in the world, then the redemptive process can work.[22]

Through the interpretive lens of a boundary-breaking Jesus who aligns with the disinherited, Thurman committed his life to releasing spiritual energy that unsettled systems as a course of social action. So, too, are the contributors in the third section armed with radical perspectives of Jesus and devoted to social change. In their work and life, Stephen Lewis, Marian Wright Edelman, Starsky D. Wilson, and Liza Rankow release a swell of spiritual energy in advocating for children, combating police brutality, counseling activists, and reframing theological education, respectively.

Born in the sticky heat of Atlanta, the shading of King's legacy fell upon all youth one generation removed from the civil rights movement. I literally stood in the shadows of giants, as my father—the accountant—kept the books of civil rights icons, Atlanta's mayors, and Black college presidents. On Saturdays, my mother, the educator, volunteered at the Southern Christian Leadership Conference's head-quarters, where our pastor, Rev. Dr. Joseph Lowery, served as president. I'll never forget sitting a stone's throw from President Nelson Mandela when he visited our church during his post-incarceration tour of Atlanta. In my youth, giants surrounded me. This did not change in adulthood, as I held court with scholar-activists, prophetic ministers, and members of the Black Lives Matter community. Though I was reared under shade trees planted by civil rights icons and I shared water with contemporary change agents from the academy, church, and the streets, in their company I did not fit. Again, Thurman proved an anchor to help me frame how my unique skill set of releasing healing energy might be a vehicle for social change.

THURMAN AS SPIRITUAL ANCHOR

While he was on leave as chairman of the Negro Delegation of Friend-ship to India, Howard University appointed Thurman as dean of Rankin Chapel. Constructed in 1894, the ivy-covered Rankin Memorial Chapel was the only auditorium on campus and doubled as a multi-purpose facility for concerts, lectures, and general campus-community meetings.[23] However, under Thurman's leadership the multiuse audi-torium became known as a sacred space where "race, sex, culture, mate-rial belongings, and religious orientation became undifferentiated in the presence of God."[24] Operating with the belief that "the life of the spirit among different people had essentially the same needs," from 1932 through 1944 Thurman "experimented with the arts, medita-tions, and innovative liturgies . . . to override conditions and beliefs that divide" communities.[25] Yet, in his twelfth year at Howard Univer-sity, Thurman sought a larger laboratory to test his dream that Chris-tianity might overcome the "separateness of discrimination, prejudice, and segregation."[26]

In the summer of 1944, Thurman took an unpaid yearlong leave of absence from Howard University and accepted the invitation of Rev. Alfred G. Fisk to cofound and copastor the Church for the Fellowship of All Peoples. Many of Thurman's closest friends and colleagues ques-tioned his decision to depart the prestigious post as dean at the most renowned historically Black university to travel cross-country and start a church with meager funds. Yet, years before Fisk's invitation, Thur-man had a spiritual epiphany that alerted him to a vocational change on the horizon. While on the Negro delegation's visit to the Khyber Pass in Pakistan, Thurman looked out over the expanse that for centuries had been rife with border wars, and he envisioned a new way:

> We knew that we must test whether a religious fellowship could be developed in America that was capable of cutting across all racial barriers, with a carry-over into the common life, a fellowship that would alter the behavior patterns of those involved. It became imperative now to find out if experiences of spiritual unity among people could be more compelling than the experiences which divide them.[27]

With the dream of unity long implanted in his heart, Thurman and his family embarked upon a bold adventure in San Francisco as they launched with Fisk "the first church in America that was interracial in its membership and leadership."[28]

Though small in size, the Fellowship Church had profound effects on Thurman's ministry. Fluker actually refers to Thurman's decade at the Fellowship Church as "the apex of his career," for in these years Thurman published regularly, his message expanded beyond the reach of his immediate admirers, and he garnered national recognition as a spiritual leader.[29] So vast was his reach that in 1953, *Life* magazine acclaimed Howard Thurman one of the twelve Great Preachers in the United States.[30] Named alongside religious icons like William "Billy" Graham and Norman Vincent Peale, Thurman—the only African American named in the group—was lauded as a religious pioneer. Shortly after the magazine's publication, Thurman left his post at the Fellowship Church and returned to academia where he became Boston University's dean of Marsh Chapel and professor in the school of theology.

As dean, Thurman continued the liturgical experiments he started in San Francisco. Thurman envisioned the university chapel as a "non-creedal, non-sectarian, interracial, interfaith and intercultural religious fellowship."[31] To test this religious theory, Thurman largely stripped the Sunday service of parochially Christian elements. Yet, through preaching and periods of meditation, he invited people of all backgrounds to deepen the authentic lines of their spiritual quest.[32] One Hindu student commented, "I have never heard a Christian preacher who could be put on the same level of spiritual understanding as the great Swamis of India."[33] So, too, did law student Barbara Jordan, who would become a congresswoman, frequent the chapel. She recounted,

"How Thurman was outstanding. . . . His sermons were focused upon the present time that all of us were having difficulty coming to grips with." A theology student at the university named Martin Luther King Jr. also "attended Marsh Chapel, listened carefully, and shook 'his head in amazement at Thurman's deep wisdom.'"[34] Thurman led Marsh Chapel until his retirement in 1965; for the remainder of his days he served as a spiritual anchor for individuals and communities in search of common ground.

Many years ago, the fertile ground of my heart seeded a dream to connect a cadre of luminaries who had grown to love the life and work of Howard Thurman. This seed was nurtured by the gifts of the Louisville Institute, Candler School of Theology, and the Children's Defense Fund. On September 16–18, 2016, the dream took root when the contributing authors in this volume gathered on the Alex Haley Farm in Clinton, Tennessee. On the open range of that greenspace, these public personalities shed their protective masks and showed up as wholly present. Guided by the arts, meditation, and innovative liturgies, together we laughed, smiled, prayed, and found authentic fellowship. On the final day, we poured libations and tears fell; never have I felt closer to heaven.

In the spirit of building common ground and creating space for authentic fellowship, the final section of this book uplifts the wisdom of a seminary president, a dean of a university chapel, a professor of preaching turned pastor, and a Christian monk turned church planter. Each has committed to creating spaces of spiritual unity. Each has found Thurman as a spiritual anchor in the current.

ANCHORED IN THE CURRENT?

"Scientists know little about the gentle upward diffusion of deep water." In one experiment, a chemical released in the depths of the Atlantic Ocean rose only sixty feet within six months and one hundred feet within one year. Many still question how the deep sea is softly stirred. Some speculate that internal waves break over hills on the sea floor to lift the deep water. Others hypothesize the distant moon tugs the tides at the surface.[35]

For Thurman, the great waters proved a divine mystery that softly stirred questions from the deep. The vastness, depth, movement, gentleness, and power of the sea became a lasting metaphor of the inner

world and life of the spirit. This fascination with the seafloor, the tug-
ging tides, and the pull of white-capped waves is evident in Thurman's
life and writing.

In boyhood, Thurman befriended the sea. He stood unafraid on the
shores of the Atlantic and watched storms roll into Daytona Beach. In
his autobiography, Thurman remembered that as the ferocious winds
billowed and the ten-foot waves dashed ashore, "the storms gave me a
certain overriding immunity against much of the pain which I would
have to deal in the years ahead."[36] At thirty, he sought the solace of
the sea on his solo journey to Europe following the death of his first
wife. Five years later, on a Pilgrimage of Friendship, he would cross
the Great Divide a second time en route to India. Aboard that seafaring vessel, Thurman described the mood of the sea as "restless," and
for days at a time the waters voiced a "pure rage." While the ship was
"flung recklessly up and down," Thurman admits, "I loved it all. The
very roots of my being were exposed by the raw energy of the sea. . . .
Not once did I sicken, not once did I miss a meal."[37]

References to the ocean's rhythm and abiding wisdom appear in one
of Thurman's soul-stirring meditations that beckons, "in every person
there is an inward sea." In several of his writings and sermons, Thurman cites a favorite poem titled "The Call of the Sea":

> I am tired of sailing my little boat
> Far inside the harbor bar—
> I want to go out where the big ships float
> Out on the deep where the great ones are.[38]

In both Thurman's devotion, "The Inward Sea" and his oft-quoted
favorite poem, an allusion may be drawn that divine wisdom and vocational understanding is accessible only to those who venture beyond
the safety of the shore. Out on the deep, mysteries unfold, questions
arise, and an attunement with the gentility and forcefulness of the Creator is made known. However, the following sea allusion in Thurman's
"Strange Freedom" inspired this book's title and has riddled many
standing far from the shoreline. "It is a strange freedom to be adrift
in the world . . . without a sense of anchor anywhere. Always there
is the need of mooring, the need for the firm grip on something that
is rooted and will not give." What makes this freedom strange? How
must it feel to be adrift in the world? Why the need for mooring? Why
drop anchor in the current? To landlocked minds the imagery of being

adrift, unmoored, and unanchored in surging waters may mean little. This was not the case for the young folk I met in Hatchet Bay. Far from the sandy resort beaches of Nassau, Hatchet Bay is a rural working-class community on one of the Bahamas' family islands. This town and its peoples lived with an unshakable stigma. When I visited in 2013, the chicken plantation on Hatchet Bay's grounds had been closed for nearly forty years. Yet, decades later the people of this proud community were still being likened with the stench and filth of the bird plantation. Strikingly, its children and youth were ridden with stigmatizing labels that foreshadowed prostitution, imprisonment, and addiction. In their company we read and discussed Thurman's "Strange Freedom." These young and inquisitive minds immediately clung to the words "anchor," "mooring," and "adrift." As the angry sea rushed against rocks one hundred feet away from our building, they taught me that an unanchored boat will be lost to the tide. If that boat is unmoored—not tied down—during the current, a family's livelihood and ability to fish for food is compromised. To be adrift and unconnected to a steadying source compromises survival.

For many, Thurman has been an anchor, a place of mooring on the seas of life. We offer this anchor to you. As you begin this book, uncertainties around vocation, education, activism, and spirituality may be sending you in a whirl and misdirecting your route. For this reason, grounding questions close each chapter. Heed the wisdom of Luther Smith's afterword and quest with these questions. Do not rush to answer. Instead, love these questions. Live them fully, and as Elesa Commerse beckons in her postlude stay readied for the unexpected.[39]

Finally, beloved reader, the time has come. Feel the tides surge beneath as you launch out on the inward sea. Use this book as your seafaring guide. Chart your course of new beginnings; see vocation afresh. Map out fresh ideas on education to keep your ship aright. When the sun sets on the horizon and the night blankets the deep, look to the stars, and there you'll find where spirituality and social action align. And in the coming dawn of day, if a storm lingers near, move with the winds of spirit that seek a common truth. And should you start to drift off course, look beneath the stern, where you'll find an anchor in the current, an eternal wisdom for this changing world. Peace for the journey.

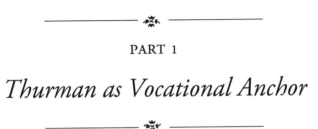

PART 1

Thurman as Vocational Anchor

Interlude
Our Life and Times

MARI EVANS

This is a cautionary tale
For parents and caregivers
Living in the midst of joy and wonder
Subliminally unconscious

The oldest was,
from his beginning,
    chivalrous . . .

The youngest was,
from his beginning,
    Love, personified . . .

We listened, we heard their voices
we did not understand, or know
what they were saying; We watched
but did not understand what we
were seeing . . .

    Innocence adrift
Innocents adrift in childhood's chaos
    Childhood's turbulence
    Childhood's vulnerability
        and we the sea
            We the sea . . .

Living in the midst of joy and wonder
with no understanding; in the midst
of fear and apprehension
    Subliminally unconscious

Too deaf and much too blind
    to see or feel
        the pain

1

Longing for Reunion with a Man
I Never Met

BARBARA BROWN TAYLOR

To love is to make of one's heart a swinging door.
—Howard Thurman, *Disciplines of the Spirit*[1]

My relationship with Howard Thurman is so unbound by time that I cannot tell you how or when it began. Many of the copies of his books on my shelf have my maiden name inside them, which suggests a connection of forty years or more. But did I meet him in college or seminary? His face is as familiar as King's or Gandhi's. But who introduced him to me? The trademark cadence of his voice quiets any crowd. But how did I miss hearing it live? Like all the important relationships in my life, this one has no evident beginning or end. Love makes of the heart a swinging door, with no clocks on either side.

When I left parish ministry for the classroom in 1997, Thurman's portrait had hung in my virtual art gallery for so long that the paint had weathered around it. I thought of him the same way I thought of George Washington Carver, Ida B. Wells, or W. E. B. Du Bois, as a luminary who belonged to other people first. He was an African American genius on whom African Americans had primary claim, not least because they received his teachings on violence, suffering, and reconciliation in ways I never could. My white life was so different from his and theirs that I kept a respectful distance, happy for the crumbs that fell from the table. I overheard what Thurman said above my head and was grateful to be in the room at all.

The last thing I expected was to meet him again in a world religions class in rural north Georgia, but that is what happened. I had added a new textbook to the syllabus called *My Neighbor's Faith: Stories of Interreligious Encounter, Growth and Transformation*.[2] One of the first-person essays in the book was by Rabbi Zalman Schachter-Shalomi, a prominent leader of the worldwide Jewish Renewal movement. When he was invited to write about a significant encounter with someone of another faith, he remembered something that had happened much earlier in his life, when he first became a graduate student at Boston University in 1955.

Reb Zalman was in his early thirties then, serving an Orthodox congregation in New Bedford, Massachusetts. His entire religious education up to that point had taken place within the Jewish world. When he felt called to study the psychology of religion in the wider world, the first thing he did was to ask for his rebbe's permission to enter the master's program at BU. Then he started figuring out how to handle the commute from New Bedford to Boston.

As an Orthodox rabbi, he was committed to saying morning prayers as close to sunrise as possible, which would have posed no problem during the summer months. He could have said his prayers at home before entering the rush hour stream of traffic toward Boston. But since his classes began in the winter, he had to come up with a different plan. The only one that worked was to leave home at 5:00 a.m. while it was still dark, watch the sun rise on his way to school, arrive on campus in time to say his prayers, and have breakfast before his first class at 8:00 a.m.

What he had not yet worked out was *where* to pray. The Hillel House on campus was not open when he arrived. Next he tried the main university chapel, which *was* open, but too full of Christian images for his Orthodox Jewish comfort. After that he went downstairs and discovered a small meditation chapel, but it was dominated by a large brass cross on an altar that still left him feeling crowded. Finally he found an open door to the Daniel Marsh Memorabilia Room, where he settled in an east-facing corner and began praying toward Jerusalem. This worked well enough that the room became his regular destination on his early mornings in Boston.

He was in and out before 8:00 a.m., which may be why he thought the man who surprised him one day was the janitor. "I've seen you here several times," the middle-aged Black man said. "Wouldn't you like to say your prayers in the small chapel?" The man was so kind and plainspoken that Reb Zalman worried about hurting his feelings if he explained about the cross. While he was still trying to think what to say, the man looked at him earnestly and said, "Why don't you stop by the chapel tomorrow morning and take a look? Maybe you'd be comfortable saying your prayers there."

When he arrived the next morning, Reb Zalman looked in the small chapel to find the large cross gone. In its place were two candles burning in brass candlesticks, with a giant Bible between them opened to Psalm 139: "Whither shall I flee from Thy presence?"

"From then on," he wrote, "I understood that I was at liberty to move the cross and say my morning prayers in the chapel. Afterward, I would always put the cross back and turn the pages to Psalm 100, the 'thank you' psalm." He still had no idea who his host was.

A short time later, Reb Zalman learned that the Dean of the Chapel was offering a course in spiritual discipline. He was intrigued because the course included "labs," but he was also leery because he knew the Dean was a Christian who might feel obliged to try and convert him. Before registering for the course, he made an appointment to discuss his concerns.

The minute he saw the friendly Black man from the chapel sitting behind the Dean's desk, the rabbi knew his concerns had been misplaced. As he had learned from their first encounter in the chapel, this was someone he could trust. But he was still anxious about how far away from home the course might take him.

"Dean Thurman," he said, "I would like to take your course, but I don't know if my 'ANCHOR chains' are long enough." Thurman did not answer him right away. Instead, he put his coffee cup down on his desk and began to look at his own hands, turning them over and over as if he were considering two sides of an argument. One side was very light, Reb Zalman noticed, while the other side was very dark. Thurman did this for so long and with such calm that Reb Zalman had plenty of time to examine the large bump on Thurman's forehead, just above and between his eyebrows. "I could swear that it was about to open and reveal the 'third eye,'" he said, when Thurman finally spoke.

"Don't you trust the *ru'ah hakodesh*?" Thurman asked him.

Reb Zalman was stunned. "He had used the Hebrew for the Holy Spirit, something I had not expected from a Gentile. And in so doing, he brought that question home to me in a powerful way. I began to tremble and rushed out of his office without answering him."

For the next three weeks, he said, he was tormented by Thurman's question. Did he indeed trust the *ru'ah hakodesh* enough to risk an encounter with another religion—to trust his soul to a non-Jew—without fearing the loss of his Jewish identity? After he realized there was only one answer to Thurman's question, he signed up for the course, which he found "marvelous and tremendously impactful." In it, he not only learned that his trust in the Holy Spirit was well placed. He also learned from Thurman "what a living, breathing religion is all about."

INTER-RUPTIONS: SEISMIC SHIFTS AND INTERCONNECTIONS

This story caused a seismic shift in my relationship with Thurman. In the first eruption, I realized that words alone would never deliver me into his presence. I could read as many of his books as I liked, but this was not the same as watching him get up early one morning to turn a small Christian chapel into a place where a rabbi could say his prayers, taking one last look from the door to make sure the welcome was clear, and leaving without a word. I could listen to the recorded archive of his sermons, lectures, and seminars from beginning to end, but that was not the same as sitting in front of him while he turned his hands over and over again, entirely at home in the silence, until he came up with the perfect question to send his visitor away—speechless—to seek the truth.

In the second eruption, I realized that Howard Thurman could be my teacher too. His ministry was not only interracial; it was also interreligious, intercultural, interlingual, and interdisciplinary. If life had been discovered on other planets before he died, I am pretty sure his ministry would have been interplanetary too. None of this diminished his stature as an icon of the American civil rights movement or blunted the fact that the Voting Rights Act of 1965 was still twelve years in the future when he became the first Black dean at a major white university. It simply meant that he might be speaking to me, in my skin, as profoundly as he was speaking to other people in theirs.

Rediscovering Thurman in the context of a college course on world religions sent me back to the shelf of his books again. What else did he have to say to people like my students and me, who were just beginning to learn other religious languages? How could he help us see that affirming the religious identities of other people did not make us traitors to our own? None of us could say *ru'ah hakodesh* yet, but the fact that Thurman had done so in a way that changed a rabbi's life—not by converting him to Christianity, but by speaking to him in his own language about his own faith—this caused a stir. How had Thurman come to such a quiet understanding that the best way to practice his own faith was to encourage other people in theirs?

PUBLIC VOCATION, QUIET WITNESS: THURMAN AS PROPHET AND MYSTIC

The first book I chose was not one Thurman wrote, but one that was written about him: *Howard Thurman: The Mystic as Prophet* by Luther E. Smith Jr. It had been on my shelf so long that all the letters on the spine had faded from the sun. I met Smith at Candler School of Theology in the late 1970s, when he was on the faculty and I was assistant to the dean. He was an affable scholar, beloved by his students, who taught courses in church and community. He was also unfailingly kind to me, the least significant person he passed in the hallway on his way to meet his classes.

His book on Thurman came out in 1981, published by the same Quaker press that published a dozen of Thurman's titles. Over the next ten years it received such wide attention both in the academy and in the church that Smith offered a revised edition in 1991. The subtitle alone was worth the price of admission, since it wedded two words that are often opposed: mystic and prophet. But what helped me most was to have an expert guide to the remarkable scope of Thurman's life and thought, someone who could deal just as expertly with challenges to Thurman's teachings by people such as Reinhold Niebuhr and James Cone.

Reading Smith's book opened my eyes even wider to how expansive Thurman's interests and commitments were. I expected to learn more about his work for racial reconciliation and social change. What I did not expect was to rethink my own theology, ecclesiology, pedagogy, preaching, pastoral care, and spirituality in response to his.

I knew that Thurman had met with Gandhi in India in 1936, returning home with a vision of how satyagraha—the practice of nonviolent resistance—could be key to the American civil rights movement. But I did not know that he had studied with the Quaker mystic Rufus Jones as far back as 1929. I knew that he had founded the Church for the Fellowship of All Peoples with Alfred Fisk in San Francisco in 1944, often recognized as the first church in America with interracial membership and leadership. But I did not know that by the time he left that congregation in 1953, *Life* magazine had named him one of the twelve greatest preachers in the United States, the only Black man on the list.

As I kept reading Smith's book, the new information piled up. In 1960 Thurman traveled the world with his wife Sue Bailey, just two years after Pan Am introduced jetliners to its fleet. Throughout his long ministry, he spoke at synagogues and churches, university chapels and YMCAs, Girl Scout banquets and chambers of commerce. In 1965, within a space of two months, Thurman addressed the Progressive National Baptist Convention and the General Assembly of the Union of American Hebrew Congregations.

Was he ahead of his times, or are we behind ours? With all this (and a lot more) before me, it was tempting to decide that Thurman was simply too magnificent for me, that I would combust if I tried to get too close to him. But Reb Zalman's story had shown me another side of the public man, and Luther Smith gave me a frame for what I saw: Howard Thurman was a Christian mystic. Everything he said, wrote, taught, and did flowed from a single source, which was his direct and incontrovertible encounter with the Divine. That was how he discovered the Really Real, which funded his courage to challenge the unreal in all its guises: unjustness, unkindness, unreconciliation, unfreedom.

This fresh focus helped me see how Thurman's life as an activist was nourished by his life as a contemplative. If you read the chronology of his professional life, you cannot miss the mention of him suffering exhaustion in his thirties, followed by an increasing number of sabbaticals in his later years. His prophetic gifts grew during his regular withdrawals from public life. The power of his voice depended on giving it a rest. This, too, strikes me as prophetic for a culture in which everyone seems to be talking entirely too much—where many young people sleep with their smartphones, elders manage growing Twitter feeds, and those eager to establish a brand fear losing momentum if they step away from their platforms for more than a week.

Since Thurman died in 1981, before many of the words in that last sentence were invented, he had nothing to say directly about them. But he wrote something in *The Inward Journey* (1961) that had enough surplus meaning to bear repeating in *Disciplines of the Spirit* (1963). Honoring the true self is far from easy, he wrote, when there are so many claims and counterclaims upon us.

Some say, "Do this, do that,"
Or, "Give up your goods. Hold nothing back
And free yourself to find your way."
Again, "Commit your way to something good
That makes upon your life the great demand.
Place upon the altar all hopes and dreams
Leaving no thing untouched, no thing unclaimed."
And yet, no peace . . .
"What more?" I ask with troubled mind.
The answer. . . . moving stillness.
And then
The burning stare of the eyes of God
Pierces my inmost core
Beyond my strength, beyond my weakness,
Beyond what I am,
Beyond what I would be,
Until my refuge is in [God] alone.
"This . . . This above all else I claim," God says.[3]

The first time I read this, I thought Thurman was urging me to give up my possessions, hold nothing back, commit my way to something good that made upon my life a great demand. Those were such familiar calls to faith that I fully expected him to reiterate them. Didn't they describe the kind of life that he and the other great ones had lived? The second time I read it, I realized the opposite: Thurman was telling me how little peace there was in following familiar calls to faith. Even a man like him, who lived his whole life straining every nerve to do his best, could find himself at the dead end of a false road, wondering what had happened.

"What more?" the "I" of this passage wants to know. What more can a person do, who has followed the good counsel of so many different voices without arriving at a place of peace within himself? The answer does not come in a complete sentence. It is . . . moving stillness. And then the burning stare of God, piercing the inmost core. After so much striving, the *more* arrives as *less*: being still, being seen, being perforated by God—borne beyond all ability, all frailty, all present and future tense, into the sole refuge of God's own being. "This is what sends a man [woman] knocking at many doors until at last he [she] finds one—a central door," Thurman wrote, "over which his [her] own name is written."[4]

The mystical way has always been difficult to defend, especially to those who are still busy "doing this, doing that." It sounds passive, for one thing, though even a cursory study of mystics such as Teresa of Avila, John Woolman, Dorothy Day, or Dom Helder Camara reveals their central roles in revolutionary social and religious reforms. It is also difficult to describe. Those who try to write about their direct experiences of God often resort to ellipses, as Thurman did. To meet the burning stare of the eyes of God has a way of vaporizing language, so that mystics are often left with little to say about the Really Real that sustains their lives in union with all other lives.

INNER LANDMARKS, SACRED GROVES, AND THE TOSSING SEA: DIRECT EXPERIENCE OF THE DIVINE

Once, when Thurman was a boy living in Daytona Beach, he walked alone along the edge of the ocean one night. "I held my breath against the night and watched the stars etch their brightness on the face of darkened canopy of the heavens," he wrote. "I had the sense that all things, the sand, the sea, the stars, the night, and I were one *lung* through which all of life breathed."[5] If you have never had that experience, he could not have explained it to you, any more than he could have explained why he first felt the unity of all living things while leaning against an old live oak tree in his back yard as a boy. Direct experience is difficult to communicate, even when it communicates the most important Reality of all.

Since nature mysticism is a familiar feature of contemporary spirituality, it is worth mentioning what sets Thurman's experience apart. He was a sensitive child who suffered a great deal from the violence of racial conflict in the South, he said. Even in Daytona Beach, where things were slightly better because of the regular influx of tourists from other parts of country, he never escaped the fear of being "brutalized, beaten, or otherwise outraged."[6] In an effort to keep this fear from running his life, he turned to God in prayer, spending more and more time alone in the woods, by the river, or on the beach. There he found the kind of freedom that he could not find in town, along with a sense of his true self—what was Really Real in him—that no one could beat out of him. There was nothing romantic about his love of nature, in other words. It was where he went to escape the fists.

Thurman's direct experience of the divine puts him in communion with other visionaries on the mystical way. So does his unorthodox theology, which departs from the orthodox version in significant—and for me, redeeming—ways. I say this knowing how vigorously he resisted being called a theologian, since he believed that religious experience was too dynamic to be organized into a system of beliefs. "Doctrinal beliefs are an important part of theology," he wrote, "but they are not the heart of it."[7] The heart of it is open to the continual newness of religious experience, which cannot be codified without compromising its vitality.

My own heart beat faster when I read that. In the language of this volume, I had found my inner landmark, though it felt more like a sacred grove to me. I wanted to walk under those trees with Thurman, learning from him how to trust my religious experience more than I feared being expelled from the community of Christians who judged it inadequate or aberrant in some way. My relationship with Jesus was so fluid that it did not depend on the virgin birth, full divinity, miraculous powers, or atoning death that were linchpins for other Christians. When I discovered the depths of Thurman's own fluid relationship with Jesus, it felt like salvation to me.

UNORTHODOX VIEWS OF CHRIST: JESUS AS RELIGIOUS SUBJECT, NOT RELIGIOUS OBJECT

I do not pretend to be a scholar of the Thurman corpus. That would take a lifetime, and a mind more rigorous than mine. I am also aware that my attraction to his work practically guarantees that I will appropriate parts of it for my own purposes, which are bound to be different from his. As inevitable as this seems for any teacher whose teachings are received by second- and third-generation students, I apologize ahead of time to my dear teacher Howard Thurman for anything I am about to say that might make him wince.

Certain teachings of his confirm instincts that have long guided my Christian thought and practice. Among the most important is his distinction between the religion *of* Jesus and the religion *about* Jesus. For reasons that had everything to do with Thurman's own social location—and the colossal failure of Christian religion to speak to people with their backs against the wall—he returned again and again to the historical Jesus, a poor Jew living in Israel under the domination of Rome. "How different might have been the story of the last two thousand years on this planet grown old from suffering," he wrote in *Jesus and the Disinherited,* "if the link between Jesus and Israel had never been severed!"

Because it *was* severed, Thurman found it necessary to return to Jesus as religious *subject* instead of religious *object,* straining to hear *his* teachings apart from the church's teaching *about* him. As difficult as this task always proves to be, it led Thurman to reclaim Jesus as someone whose entire life was about communicating "a technique of survival for the oppressed."[8] It also led him to an unorthodox view of Jesus, whom Thurman did not see as God but as the "for instance" of the mind of God. Yes, Thurman asserted, Jesus was fully human and fully divine, but there was no more God in him than in any man or woman. He was born as we are born. What set him apart was his greater consciousness of his divinity, which emerged from his closer relationship with God. His anguishing death was not engineered by God to redeem humankind; it was the demonstration of what happens to love in the world. The message of his resurrection is that the meaning of his life cannot be killed. The essence of Jesus' life, embodied in his teachings, remains alive in the world today.

In Thurman's view, God alone is absolute, and God alone is to be worshiped. Jesus shows the way to the Source of life, but he is not the Source. He is the beloved exemplar, the love-ethic come to life. He is the one who inspires us, not the one who takes our place. Watching Jesus climb the ladder will never lead us to our own intimacy with God. If we want to receive the full impact of his teaching, we will put our feet on the ladder too. We will go where Jesus went; we will seek what he sought. In Thurman's terms, we will risk a great deal for the kind of unity with God that brings us into unity with all our neighbors, increasing our resolve to confront the structures that put people's backs against the wall.

This summary does not include the "why" of Thurman's Christology, nor did he ever claim it was the whole story. He left a great deal unsaid, much of it central to orthodox Christian theology. According to Smith, there is no evidence that Thurman ever made reference to Jesus' miracles, his special birth, his sacrifice for human sin, his bodily resurrection, or his eternal life in heaven. Most astonishingly of all (although perhaps not so astonishing in light of John 14:12), Thurman suggested that Jesus may have died before his full potential had been realized, leaving other seekers to cover spiritual territory that Jesus had not gotten to yet.[9]

Why is this "Life of Christ" so important? Let me count the ways. First, because it weds the direct experience of God to concrete acts of human resistance. Second, because too many people mistake going to church for following Jesus. Waves of young people have followed him right out the door, while their elders have become exhausted with the business of institutional preservation. Young or old, those who set off in search of new spiritual territory can feel like they are leaving Jesus behind, since church teaching has convinced them that Jesus belongs to the church instead of the other way around. Thurman's unorthodox view of Jesus (along with his realistic view of church collusion in domination) opens up new and liberating ways of conceiving Christian faithfulness and purpose.

But there is another virtue to Thurman's low Christology, which is the way it lowers boundaries between Christians and those of other faiths. When Thurman cofounded Fellowship Church in 1944, the healing of racial division was topmost in his mind. Acting on a vision he had received in the mountains between Afghanistan and what was then West Pakistan, he wanted "to find out whether experiences of spiritual unity among people could be more compelling than the experiences which divide them."[10] He knew all too well how many churches operated on the principle of exclusion based on color, creed, economics, or culture. He wanted Fellowship Church to be a place where people with different understandings of Jesus could come together with people who were not sure how they felt about him at all.

TO LIVE AT ODDS: THURMAN'S INTIMACY WITH THE REALLY REAL

For Thurman, a fellowship truly open to all peoples meant that belief in Jesus-as-God could not be a prerequisite for inclusion. By focusing on Jesus-as-Human-Exemplar instead, he hoped to meet Christians in all the varieties of their faith without alienating people of other faiths who were drawn to Fellowship Church. He also gave legs to his conviction that the Christian church comes into its own completeness when people of other faiths are fully integrated into its community— not as converts, but as fellow seekers reminding Christians that they do not have a lock on God. Meanwhile, he fully expected the spiritual gifts to flow both ways. Any discovery that opens a new door to God, he said—through the arts, through the faith of others, through shared spiritual practices—is useful to Christians with their feet on the ladder.

I have had enough practice with thoughts like these to hear the accusatory voices rise up in my head: Gnosticism! Arianism! Relativism! Syncretism! This leads back to a third familiar feature of mystical experience, which is its failure to conform to traditional church teaching. Think of John of the Cross, imprisoned and beaten by brothers in his own religious order, or Marguerite Porète, burned at the stake by the Inquisition. Think of Brazilian archbishop Dom Helder Camara, whose liberation theology led members of his own church to urge the government to arrest him, or French activist Simone Weil, who—though drawn powerfully to Catholic Christianity—declined to be baptized in light of church teaching that there was no salvation outside the church.

In my view, the problem for all these Christian mystics and more is that their unmediated experience of the Divine puts them at odds with the traditional mediators of the divine, which include church authorities, church doctrines, church sacraments, and church polities. The intimacy of their encounters with the Really Real ends their allegiance to the multiple systems of checks and balances put in place to monitor such encounters. When they hear the call of God on their lives, the call of the systems becomes faint by comparison. If forced to choose, they choose, and some pay for their decision with their lives.

Thurman, thank God, did not. Perhaps it was his spiritual independence that saved him, or perhaps it was his temperament, leading him to a life that was more contemplative than activist. Perhaps it was his faith in the dynamism of religious experience, which freed him from having to defend his own rightness in practice or belief. Whatever it was, his unorthodox Christian faith came to public expression with a personal gentleness and theological humility that are too rare in American religious life today. He embodied his truth and trusted other people to embody theirs. He held a vision of human community through a lifetime full of reasons to give it up. He released later generations of seekers to explore the spiritual territory he had not gotten to yet, just as he believed Jesus did.

These are a few of the reasons why I claim Howard Thurman as my venerable ancestor, my posthumous mentor, my interplanetary guru and guide to a perplexing new world. While he did not say a word (as far as I know) about gender fluidity, multiple religious identity, or the millennial reinvention of evangelicalism in the twenty-first century, he knew what was Really Real, and he knew how much theological revolution might be involved in drawing nearer to that. He made of my heart a swinging door. He asked me whether I trusted the *ru'ah hakodesh*. He showed me how to put my foot on the ladder. What more could anyone ask? The rest is up to us.

GROUNDING QUESTIONS

1. If you are reading this book, you have knocked on a lot of spiritual doors by now. Which one has turned out to be central for you—the one over which your own name is written?
2. What is your most cherished failure, the one that was most helpful in refocusing your true purpose in life?
3. Suffering causes breakdown; it can also cause breakthrough. What experience of suffering in your life or the life of your community has involved both breaks?
4. How would you describe your relationship to silence? If it is something you seek, say why. If it is something you flee, say why. What is the difference between solitary silence and communal silence for you?
5. What is your strongest story of nonviolence in the face of violence? Whether it is your story or someone else's, what did you see happen when violence was absorbed instead of returned?

2

Listening for the Voice of Vocation

Hearing the Sound of the Genuine
in Solitude and Community

PARKER J. PALMER

MEETING HOWARD THURMAN

I knew very little about Howard Thurman's life and work until I was in my fifties and he was no longer with us. But as I began to read his books, he soon came to feel like an old friend. His legacy of deep-reaching words, and the commanding yet gentle presence that saints leave in the air long after they pass by, made me feel I knew him well, and he knew me.

I grew up in an all-white community of affluence and privilege, a community hermetically sealed against the richness of human diversity. Even the Methodist church my family attended—where we were taught about a God of love in whom all people are one—was not a place where we were likely to be exposed to the writings of an African American pastor raised by his former-slave grandmother among the working poor in Daytona Beach, Florida. Sadly, 11:00 a.m. on Sunday morning was and still is the most segregated hour of the week in the U.S.A., spiritually and intellectually segregated as well as bodily.

As a teenager in the 1950s, the Christian writer I heard most about was Norman Vincent Peale, whose bootstrap version of Christianity as a pathway to "success"—as defined by American culture—spoke to "my people." Compare the title of Peale's best-selling *The Power of Positive Thinking* (1952) with Thurman's *Jesus and the Disinherited* (1949) and you have a thumbnail sketch of two planets separated by light years, whose inhabitants were very unlikely to meet and talk with each other in the course of daily life.

I began to do some interplanetary traveling when I graduated from an almost all-white college in 1961. I spent a year at Union Theological Seminary in Manhattan, 1961–62. Alongside my academic studies, I was given a field work assignment at Riverside Church, working with junior high students from Spanish Harlem, and supervised by a gifted youth minister who was the first African American I came to know personally. Thus began my ongoing education in diversity.

From Union, I went to the University of California at Berkeley, where I spent five years working on a PhD in sociology in the middle of a decade of political and cultural turbulence that found vigorous expression on the Berkeley campus. I learned as much, maybe more, from what was happening in the streets—the free speech movement, the struggle against the war in Vietnam, the rise of the Black Panthers—as I learned in the classroom.

In 1969, with PhD in hand, I made my first major vocational decision, a decision that's not merely about a job but about one's larger purpose in life: I decided not to pursue a professorship but to become a community organizer in Washington, DC. My heroes had been assassinated, the cities were burning from "the fire next time," and I felt strongly called to use my sociology in the community rather than in the classroom. I spent the next five years working to help to integrate and stabilize a historically white, middle-class neighborhood that was undergoing rapid racial and socioeconomic change.

That work challenged me, body and soul. I needed spiritual sustenance that went well beyond "the power of positive thinking." I found what I needed—first in the writings of the Trappist monk Thomas Merton, and later in the faith and practice of the Religious Society of Friends (Quakers).

On the surface, these two spiritual sources would seem to have little or nothing in common: a Trappist living by rigorous monastic vows under the hierarchical order of the Roman Catholic Church, and a Christian sect that has no creed, no clergy, no sacraments. But despite their external differences, Merton and the Quakers modeled a way of joining the inward journey and the outward reach that some have called "ethical mysticism"—words that, I later learned, could also be used to describe Howard Thurman's way of engaging the world.[1]

During the 1970s, Thurman was on my radar only peripherally. But in the 1980s—as my involvement in social change deepened and my spiritual quest grew more intense—my awareness of his importance grew. African American friends and colleagues whom I respected and admired helped me understand how Thurman's spirituality had animated their lives, as it had animated the ministry of Martin Luther King Jr. I have since learned that Dr. King carried two books with him everywhere he went: the Holy Bible and *Jesus and the Disinherited*.

By the end of the 1980s, it became clear to me that Howard Thurman, Thomas Merton, and the Quakers represented different takes on what some have called "the perennial wisdom." It also became clear that the life experience from which Thurman spoke and wrote would open new interpretations of that wisdom for people like me who are white, relatively affluent, and privileged. I began to see that if I were to continue to care about and work for justice in a nation whose racism runs DNA-deep, the life and work of Howard Thurman could provide some of the "gene therapy" both I and my country needed in order to survive and thrive.

JOINED BY THE LIVING WATER: FACING THE ANCIENT QUESTIONS OF VOCATION

From 1974 to 1985, I lived and worked at a Quaker living-learning community/adult study center near Philadelphia called Pendle Hill, founded in 1930. I did not know it at the time, but two of Pendle Hill's founders—Rufus Jones and Douglas Steere of Haverford College—were among Howard Thurman's teachers and conversation partners, making his resonance with Quakerism more than accidental.[2] Thurman testified to the centrality of this connection in a 1961 essay he published in the Pendle Hill Pamphlet series:

> In 1929, I was a special student with Rufus Jones at Haverford College. He gave to me confidence in the insight that the religion of the inner life could deal with the empirical experience of [humanity] without retreating from the demands of such experience. To state what I mean categorically, the religion of the inner life at its best is life affirming rather than life denying. . . .[3]

A daily feature of life at Pendle Hill was Quaker meeting for worship, a form of worship grounded in silence, in which members of the "gathered community" sometimes feel led by the Spirit to speak spontaneously. One morning a woman spoke words that immediately rang true for me. I believe that they would have rung true for Howard Thurman, as well:

> Many of us seek unity amid human diversity. But we seem to think that the way to get there is "upward," into abstraction, where our differences get blurred and we can harbor the illusion that we are one. But instead of becoming one, we lose our identities, our unique stories, and cannot forge meaningful relationships because we do not show up as who we are.
>
> The way to unity is not up into abstraction but down into particularity. If each of us will go deep enough into our own story, into the well of our own experience, we will find ourselves drinking from the same aquifer of living water that feeds all the wells. That's where true unity is to be found. . . .

As I began dipping, then diving into Thurman's work, I found point after point where it was clear that he, Merton, and the Quakers were doing exactly what that Friend had spoken about in meeting. They were drilling deep into the wells of diverse life experiences, expressed in their own native tongues, and drawing up the same living water to quench the spiritual thirst of countless people.

One of the best examples of this is found in the way Merton, the Quakers, and Thurman address the ancient question of vocation, posed by the prophet Ezekiel (33:10) when he asked, "How then shall we live?"

During my early days as a community organizer, I'd been drawn to Merton's edgy claim that "most of us live lives of self-impersonation." Caught between conflicting guidance from within and without, tainted by ego and tempted by a culture of materialism, I feared falling into fraudulence as I sought to understand what God was calling me to do with my life, given my gifts and the self-evident needs of the world around me.

Fortunately, Merton had more than irony to offer! He wrote about the primal reality of what he called "true self"—a God-given self that cuts through the ego's illusions about who we are, what gifts we possess, and how our gifts might best serve a suffering world. True self, he argued, is the ultimate guide when it comes to charting a path of meaning and purpose.

Quaker tradition has its own version of Merton's "true self." It goes by various names—"the Inner Teacher," "the Inner Light," "the Indwelling Christ"—and is one of the foundational elements of

Quaker faith and practice. Each of us, say the Quakers, has "that of God" within us, a core of human selfhood, of personal identity and integrity, that offers us the best guidance available—if we can hear its still, small voice amid the cacophony within and around us.

Howard Thurman spoke of this still, small voice as "the sound of the genuine" in every person, a phrase he used in the baccalaureate address he delivered at Spelman College on May 4, 1980, a year before he died. These are the words through which I first encountered Thurman at some point in the late 1990s, words that spoke so deeply to me that this man whom I had never met immediately felt like an old friend:

> There is something in every one of you that waits, listens for the genuine in yourself—and if you cannot hear it, you will never find whatever it is for which you are searching and if you hear it and then do not follow it, it was better that you had never been born. You are the only you that has ever lived; your idiom is the only idiom of its kind in all the existences, and if you cannot hear the sound of the genuine in you, you will all of your life spend your days on the ends of strings that somebody else pulls.[4]

For obvious reasons, Thurman's emphasis on listening for "the sound of the genuine" resonated with insights I'd gained from Merton and the Quaker tradition. But beyond reinforcing this familiar notion, Thurman's words carried a prophetic edge that sharpened and clarified my fear of living a life of "self-impersonation"—a life guided by a "fraudulent self" or a "false inner teacher." I'm referring to the hard truths he spoke about the price we pay for ignoring or defying the sound of the genuine in us.

Defy the genuine, Thurman says, and you will "spend your days on the ends of strings that somebody else pulls." Those words affirmed me as I looked back on my younger self, determined to find my own way amid a welter of voices calling me to walk paths that weren't my own.

As a young man, I was surrounded by mentors who were certain I was destined to move quickly up the academic ranks and, in record time, become a young college president. But as soon as I finished my PhD, I left academia, followed my own sense of calling into community organizing, and never looked back. Of course, I was full of fear about hacking an uncharted path through the world—one that had no "career ladder" and often no predictable paycheck. But I treasured the freedom that came from "cutting the strings."

Defy the genuine, Thurman says, and "it was better that you had never been born."[5] Strong words, those. But if I found them a bit over-stated, even shocking when I first read them twenty years ago, they make perfect sense to me today at age eighty-one.

I've lived long enough to become acutely aware of my own mortality, not morbidly, but in a way that enhances my gratitude for the gift of life. From the vantage point of age, I can't imagine a sadder way to die than with the realization that I never showed up in the world as my true self. We are given only one chance to live, learn, and serve in this world as the unique "idiom" each of us is—the unique voice that speaks in us and through us, the Word made flesh in you and in me.

What could possibly be sadder than dying with the knowledge that I wasted my chance to offer the world the one-of-a-kind gift I was created to be?

WINNOWING THE CHAFF: DISCIPLINES OF VOCATIONAL DISCERNMENT

As we seek to live our lives as the God-given gifts they are, and find our authentic callings in a world of endless need, Howard Thurman, Thomas Merton, and the Quaker tradition call us to follow "the sound of the genuine," "the voice of true self," and "the pathway illumined by the inner light."

It all sounds right and good, and it is. But *how* are we to follow their advice? That question becomes daunting when we face the fact that within us we have a great many voices that do not utter "the sound of the genuine," voices that are not that of true self, voices that call us toward things that shimmer with allure but are not the inner light. Here lies the nub of the problem of vocational discernment.

As every self-reflective adult knows, none of us is a psychological or spiritual monolith, none of us speaks in a single voice. Inwardly, we are like crowded, noisy cities where many voices clamor for our attention: voices of ego, fear, anger, pain, jealousy, greed, and dozens of other distorting emotions, right alongside voices of truth, love, justice, and mercy. It's no easy thing to listen to a powerful voice—such as one that calls for revenge against a person who has done us grievous harm—and respond, "I will not do what you demand, because yours is not the sound of the genuine in me."

At the moment it speaks in white-hot anger from the heart of our own suffering, the voice of revenge can sound as genuine as genuine can be. In that moment, it does little good to recite pious platitudes like, "Love and forgiveness are the answer," as true as those words may be.

How can we home in on the voice that is sounding "the genuine" within us, telling us foundational truths about who we are—and are called to be—that will set us on a path toward fulfilling the promise of the life with which we've been graced? Between Thurman, Merton, and the Quakers, we can draw at least two vital lessons about ways of winnowing the chaff from the wheat and discerning the vocation to which we are called.

First, we can learn the importance of solitary and communal silence, that most elemental of all spiritual practices. For Thurman, Merton, and the Quakers—to say nothing of all the other wisdom teachers and traditions I know anything about—silence is foundational to all spiritual discernment.

Merton spent most of his adult life in a Trappist monastery where silence is such a prominent feature of communal life that workaday communication is conducted with hand signals in order to maintain the quietude in which one might be able to hear the "still, small voice."

Quaker meeting for worship involves people gathering in silence with no worship leader, no order of worship, and no sacred music. Members of the meeting simply wait on "that of God" moving within and among them, creating stirrings and urgings that are sometimes spoken aloud in what Quakers call "vocal ministry."

For Thurman, prayer is key to vocational discernment—and silence is the *sine qua non* of prayer. As Thurman writes,

> . . . prayer . . . means the *method* by which the individual makes his [her] way to the temple of quiet within his [her] own spirit and the *activity* of his [her] spirit within its walls. Prayer is not only the participation in communication with God in the encounter of religious experience, but it is also the "readying" of the spirit for such communication. It is the total process of quieting down and to that extent must not be separated from meditation. Perhaps, as important as prayer itself, is the "readying" of the spirit for the experience.[6]

For those of us who seek inner truth, the need for silence is self-evident, a silence that might be likened to night falling over the city, causing the clamor to cease for a while. Most of us experience such silence as respite and relief—so why do many of us have a hard time practicing silence with regularity in our daily lives? Yes, we live in a noisy world. Yes, we are busy people. But those are poor excuses for failing to carve out the conditions that would give the inner truth we seek a chance to bubble up from that great aquifer of wisdom on which every well of life draws.

The difficulty comes, I think, from the fact that most of us fear silence at least as much as we yearn for it, for at least two reasons. First, silence forces us to listen to all the voices within us that are not genuine but inauthentic, not true but false, not of the light but of the darkness. Before we can hear "the sound of the genuine" in us, we must listen to all the sounds of self-deception within us and summon the courage to tell them that they do not represent the best of who we are. That's a task no one embraces with gladness!

If we have the courage to take that task on, and manage to succeed at it, we then confront a second fear: When we hear the voice of true self speak, what might we learn about ourselves and the work to which we're called both inwardly and outwardly? I'm sure I'm not the only person who's had moments when my "inner whiner" has muttered, "I wish I'd never listened to true self. All it's done is to take me down a demanding path with many obstacles." In the long run, of course, the rewards of responding to the sound of the genuine in ourselves far outweigh the challenges.

In addition to the importance of silence in vocational discernment, there's a second lesson to be learned from Thurman, Merton, and the Quakers regarding how to home in on the sound of the genuine in us: Our silence must be surrounded by the resources of community. In community we can test our sense that "this is the sound of the genuine in me" by sharing it with others who may hear things we don't. In community we can find support in taking the often risky step of acting on what we hear from "true self" in ways that take us out of our comfort zone even as they are taking us toward the light.

Thomas Merton spent twenty-seven years, exactly half his life, living in community—the tight-knit and closely ordered community of the Abbey of Gethsemani in Kentucky. Though he often grew restive with the clear, firm boundaries of monastic life, he credited his life in community with helping him maintain his vocation, with shoring up his courage to keep seeking God even when God appeared to be unhearing, unresponsive, and unreachable. He credited the communal disciplines of the monastery with teaching him what it means to love truly and well.

For Quakers, learning in community is as pivotal to the spiritual quest as learning from the inner teacher in solitude and silence.

Quakerism is a form of organized religion with no ordained clerical leadership. So everything done by, with, or through the clergy in a traditional Christian church must be done by, with, or through community in a Quaker meeting.

For example, when someone needs pastoral counseling on a question of personal importance, such as vocation, where do you turn when there is no pastor to turn to? Early in its history, Friends developed a communal process called the Clearness Committee. The ground rules or spiritual disciplines of this process give people a way to help a fellow Quaker hear the voice of the inner teacher without presuming that *they* know what his or her inner teacher is saying.

Boiled down to its essence, the Clearness Committee is a form of community governed by two nonnegotiable rules: (1) As the members of the committee listen to the "focus person" explore the issue at hand, they may not attempt in any way to fix, save, advise, or correct that person about what he or she is saying. (2) Committee members may address the focus person only by asking *honest, open questions*—questions whose sole intent is to help the focus person enter into a deepening dialogue with his or her inner teacher, so that "the sound of the genuine" will become clearer and more audible to that person.[7]

Though Howard Thurman did not write about community in operational detail, there is no question of its importance in his thinking and his practice. As Luther Smith writes, "The major themes in Howard Thurman's spirituality are the significance of religious experience, the hunger for community, and the realization of a true sense of self."[8]

Creating as well as writing about community was central to Thurman's work as dean of Rankin Chapel at Howard University, as dean of Marsh Chapel at Boston University, and as the cofounder of the Church for the Fellowship of All Peoples in San Francisco. In every instance, I suspect, the community in question revolved around the gifts of Howard Thurman himself. But these communities were not so-called cults of personality. As many people have testified, Thurman's very presence directed people beyond himself toward the God in whose service he lived.

I've also heard a great deal of testimony that Thurman's way of being one-on-one with people carried the same kind of charge as the Quaker Clearness Committee. In this form of community, or communion, the seeker is not told what to think, what to believe, what to do. Instead, he or she is helped to listen inwardly for the sound of the genuine in him- or herself by means of penetrating questions.

As Jesse Jackson has said, "I shall forever cherish the moments seated at [Howard Thurman's] feet and listening to his searing questions that continue to haunt me in search of my truest and most authentic self."[9] Conversations with Thurman were, in effect, the "community of discernment" many people need. Community, or communion, doesn't require a throng. It can and does happen powerfully between two people.

LIVING THE QUESTIONS

As this exploration of Howard Thurman, listening for "the sound of the genuine," and discerning vocation comes to an end, I want to pose a few reflection questions in hopes of helping the reader take next steps. But instead of asking questions that might lead directly to answers, I want to ask questions of the sort inspired by the poet Rainer Maria Rilke.

In *Letters to a Young Poet*, Rilke offers this counsel to a young man who wrote him seeking vocational guidance:

> . . . be patient toward all that is unsolved in your heart and to try to love the questions themselves like locked rooms and like books that are written in a very foreign tongue. Do not now seek the answers, which cannot be given you because you would not be able to live them. And the point is, to live everything. Live the questions now. Perhaps you will then gradually, without noticing it, live along some distant day into the answer.[10]

Howard Thurman clearly believed in questions of this kind—questions that are too big to yield immediate answers. Thurman was a practitioner of "ethical mysticism" who understood that we live amid mysteries that will forever evade our full understanding—not least the mysteries of God, the human self, community, and our callings to service in a suffering world.

In that spirit, I want to pose three questions that are, I hope, worthy of wrapping one's life around—worthy of living into in hopes of living into an answer on "some distant day."

1. The first question is one I began asking before I knew I was asking it! In my late twenties and early thirties, when friends asked me why I had walked away from a secure academic career to embark on the risky

path of community organizing, the only answer I could come up with was, "This is something I *can't not do*."

As confusing as that double negative may be, it tells the truth. I was not full of enthusiasm about taking multiple risks by departing a well-marked path through the woods to hack a path of my own through the underbrush. I feared that I could not make a decent living for myself and my growing family, feared that I would fall off the radar of those who were on the look for promising young leaders, feared that I would wake up some day lost in a trackless wilderness and realize I had made a terrible and irredeemable mistake.

And yet, looking back, I realize that that double negative has been one of the most reliable vocational guides I've ever had. So, I'm going to turn it into a question for the reader, one that might prove useful in discerning vocation: **As you think about next steps on your vocational path, is there anything that you *can't not do*?**

2. When I decided to leave academia and become a community organizer, I had to make the daunting decision to lay down one vision I'd held for my life in order to pursue another. As Robert Frost says in his famous poem, "The Road Not Taken,"

> Two roads diverged in a wood, and I—
> I took the one less traveled by,
> And that has made all the difference.

Every time I've come to a vocational crossroad—and I've come to many—I've asked myself, "What do I want to let go of, and what do I want to hang onto?" It's not a bad question, but not long ago I realized that the second part of the question was less than fully life-giving. The question of what I want to "hang onto" has a fearful, clingy air about it, as if what I need is in scarce supply and I must hoard whatever I have lest I end up without enough.

So with the help of a Clearness Committee, I took a deeper dive into "the sound of the genuine" in me, and came up with a better question, which I want to offer the reader: **What do I want to let go of, and what do I want to *give myself to*?** The revised second half of that question now reflects a sense of abundance and generosity, qualities that Howard Thurman had in abundance, qualities that I aspire to embody in my vocation and my life.

3. If your vocational path is one that leads toward high values, such as love, truth, and justice, you will find yourself on a journey that never reaches its destination. Think of anyone you respect and admire for

having lived a life dedicated to values such as those. Then ask yourself, "Was that person able to die thinking, 'I'm certainly glad I devoted my life to love, truth, and justice, because now everyone on earth can take those things off his or her to-do list for all time'?"

Of course, the answer is no. The task of creating the Beloved Community has to be taken up anew in every generation, as if no one had ever tried to do it before—a fact that raises an important question about vocation: **In the end, what's more important to you: being effective and getting results or being faithful?**

We all care about results, of course, and we work hard for whatever progress we can make. But with the big tasks that God gives us, there are no final results—and if we live in hope of them, we will die in despair. So those of us who are committed to high values must have a standard that supersedes effectiveness. The name of that standard, I think, is "faithfulness."

As a way of encouraging us to live our lives fully and well, St. Benedict said, "Daily, keep your death before your eyes." If we can die saying to ourselves, "I never reached the Promised Land, but to the best of my ability, I was faithful to my gifts, to the needs I saw around me, and to the places where my gifts might serve those needs," then, I believe, we can die with a sense of satisfaction that we took what God gave us and put it in the service of life.

I have to believe that Howard Thurman died this way, faithful as he was to his lifelong calling to serve the cause of love, truth, and justice. Let us give thanks for his life, and gladly walk our own path of service through a world of suffering and joy.

GROUNDING QUESTIONS

1. As you think about next steps on your vocational path, is there anything that you *can't not do*?
2. What do I want to let go of, and what do I want to *give myself to*?
3. In the end, what's more important to you: being effective and getting results or being faithful?

---— ❧ —---

PART 2

Thurman as Anchor for Educators

---— ❧ —---

      ❧❦❧

Interlude

The Gift of Good Counsel:
Listening for "The Sound of the Genuine"

      ❧❦❧

MARTIN DOBLMEIER

The Sound of the Genuine was the title of an extraordinary address an aging Howard Thurman gave to the young women graduates at Spelman College in Atlanta in May 1980.

For me, listening for "the sound of the genuine" was an expression that immediately connected. I thought it was at once original, deeply personal yet universal. My first thought was to put myself in a place where I could be still enough to hear the echoes and guidance of my own soul. But Thurman understood that listening to oneself is only part of the equation. Thurman went on to tell the women that day, "If I hear the sound of the genuine in me and if you hear the sound of the genuine in you, it is possible for me to go down in me and come up in you. So that when I look at myself through your eyes . . . I see in me what you see in me . . . and the wall that separates and divides will disappear." For Thurman, listening for the sound of the genuine was not simply a turn of phrase or an intriguing expression. The notion was foundational for discovering the oneness of everything, and most importantly, humanity's common ground. And for those who seek transcendence in a painfully divided world, this was his roadmap to hope. But Thurman himself was able to arrive at this insight only after a lifetime of deep listening.

I came to Boston University in the late 1970s for a master's degree in broadcast journalism. It was years after Thurman had left the university where he pioneered worship and interracial community building as Dean of Marsh Chapel from 1953–1965. His imprint was still evident not only on the religious community, but across the campus. I never had the pleasure of hearing Thurman speak from the pulpit. But in the process of making a documentary film on Thurman, I listened to countless audio recordings of his sermons and public talks. I studied his classic writings, reviewed his extensive correspondence, and meditated on his evocative poetry.

Those enduring works chronicle the more public side of Howard Thurman. But there was also a more private, pastoral side of the man that deserves to be remembered and admired: in particular, his gift for deep listening. Thurman—the mystic—could not have become such an effective and prophetic voice without first mastering the art of listening.

For the film I interviewed a number of people who sought Thurman's personal counsel at critical moments in their lives. Many would travel to San Francisco to visit him during his later years when he welcomed guests regularly to his Stockton Street home. To a person they recalled being marked by the memory of a man who, despite a large public personality, relished the role of private sage, offering the wisdom of Solomon and the precious gifts of listening and good counsel.

When civil rights leader Vernon Jordan was named president of the National Urban League, he sought out Thurman. Having heard Thurman preach, Jordan was convinced that Thurman was not only a remarkable preacher but also an effective listener. Their first face-to-face meeting began at 9:00 p.m. They talked until six in the morning and promised to revisit the conversation soon. Over the next years, Jordan often came to San Francisco. Thurman had strict rules to guide their conversations. The talks would last at least three hours, and no telephones. "He was my most important mentor," Jordan remembers. "Everything was on the table with Howard Thurman. He wanted to know what was on MY mind, what was I doing? And I am eternally grateful that he was a friend of mine."

Vernon Jordan was not the only person who visited Stockton Street.

A 1978 article in *Ebony* magazine noted that "Every year scores of pilgrims—ministers, professors, students, workers, housewives, government officials—make their way to San Francisco for spiritual guidance and counseling."[1]

Thurman's only grandson, Anton Wong, remembers as a teenager seeking out his grandfather's counsel. He recalls too, needing to make an appointment because even in retirement his grandfather's schedule was so committed. "There was an appropriate time to sit with my grandfather and have a one-to-one, and there was a time when he belonged to the rest of the world," Wong said. "But you felt that when he sat down with you—you had his undivided attention." What Thurman imparted to the teen stayed with him throughout his life.

Thurman counseled the need to find the courage and determination to not let other people and situations, difficult as they may be, tear you down. Wong said he left those many sessions feeling renewed, uplifted, and most importantly, heard.

In my work as a documentary filmmaker, effective *listening* may be the most underappreciated aspect of the craft. The work involves research, coupled with technical and artistic competence. But over the years I have come to appreciate how everything starts with listening. The skill to hear both what is said and what is left unsaid is critical. I have come to recognize as well how the ability to listen deeply is a reflection of my own spiritual health and well-being. At the times when I can't hear the other person over the words being spoken in my own head, I realize how much my spiritual side needs attention. That the "genuine" in me has drifted into the disingenuous.

Hearing story after story of how Howard Thurman could offer good counsel *because* he was such a good listener only confirms how well his own spiritual center must have been ANCHORED—how, in the midst of all the public demands, he maintained a connection to what was genuine within him.

Our world bombards us with noise—voices and sounds, rhythms and beats. Just finding quiet space can be a challenge. But Thurman was not talking about simply finding quiet. He called for something more profound. He called for reaching a place of "stillness" that lets our genuine self emerge.

Most importantly, what Thurman challenged us to do was to take our own sense of spiritual security and discover how it frees us not just to acknowledge but also to honor that which is genuine in "the other"—even when the other is different from ourselves. That, Thurman understood, is the foundation for creating common ground.

3

The Inward Sea

Mapping Interior Landmarks for Leaders

WALTER EARL FLUKER

There is in every person an inward sea, and in that sea there is an island and on that island there is an altar and standing guard before that altar is the "angel with the flaming sword." Nothing can get by that angel to be placed upon that altar unless it has the mark of your inner authority. Nothing passes "the angel with the flaming sword" to be placed upon your altar unless it be a part of "the fluid area of your consent." This is your crucial link with the Eternal.

—Howard Thurman, "The Inward Sea"[1]

MEETING HOWARD THURMAN

I met Howard Thurman for the first time in the living room of my future in-laws, Agnes and Melvin Watson. Earlier I had been introduced to him through his writings while serving as a chaplain's assistant in the U.S. Army. I would later attend his lectures at Garrett-Evangelical Theological Seminary in Evanston, Illinois, and the Interdenominational Theological Center in Atlanta, Georgia, in 1979 and 1980, respectively. Imagine my surprise and delight to be in his and Sue Bailey Thurman's presence in the casual setting of my future bride's family home. What I remember most was the body-shaking laughter that emanated from this wise sage. Every moment was filled with the humor and deep wisdom that characterized his life and teachings. I would also be invited, along with nine other students who were preparing for religious vocations, to a weeklong seminar titled "Footprints of the Disinherited" held at the Howard Thurman Educational Trust in San Francisco. The seminar series would be repeated on two other occasions with African American students who, in Thurman's words, had given the "'nerve center of consent'. . . to the religious life as a personal commitment." The seminar explored "the grounds and the meaning of religious experience" and "examined the bearing of these elements on the life and the fulfillment of those of us whose roots are in the Black community." For seven days, October 21–27, 1979, we sat with this master, entranced by his long pauses and careful distillation of what it meant to devote "one's entire thought and concentration on issues that have to do not only with the meaning of life but also with the ultimate destiny of the human pilgrimage."[2] We struggled with what Thurman often referred to as the Angel with the Flaming Sword. Borrowed from George Fox's personal experience of conversion, the Angel symbolizes our existential quests and yearnings for a sense of wholeness and the unity of consciousness. The encounter with the Angel is simultaneously a trysting with the self that provides the journeyer with a new sense of identity and purpose.[3]

The time we spent together was life-changing in every sense of the word. It was one of the very few experiences in my life where I felt I was totally engaged and understood. At the risk of overstating this unique experience, I felt as if I had finally arrived "home." In fact, in Thurman's presence, poetry poured out of me like a libation to Life. Each day Thurman would begin the seminar with a scriptural passage or one of his favorite contemplative readings; once or twice he read one of his own meditations. The ten of us, six men and four women from all over the country, sat in rapt attention feasting on his every word, listening, watching, and thinking. On the first morning, wrapped in an Aztec-patterned blanket like an ancient chief in ceremonial costume, he unhurriedly sat down in a worn recliner, adjusted his body for comfort with his contorted face expressing a readiness to speak words that were yet in formation, and finally announced that he wanted to tell us a story. He asked us to imagine that we were in a café somewhere far removed from the necessities of thought and worry and to simply relax as a stranger joined us and told us this story—a story that we were hearing for the first time. Thurman proceeded to read, "The beginning of the gospel of Jesus Christ, the Son of God. As it is written in Isaiah the prophet, 'Behold, I send my messenger before your face, who will prepare your way, the voice of one crying in the wilderness: "Prepare the way of the Lord, make his paths straight."'"[4] It took the entire morning, with one break, for him to complete the story of the Gospel of Mark. His deep melodic baritone, the slow cadence and long pauses in between passages created a liminal space where insights leaped across our minds like dolphins at play in the water. After he was done, my immediate thought was that Jesus was a radically free human being; and that everything that he touched was liberated to live authentically in the world without pretense or fear. I think this was also Thurman's intention in bringing us together so that as we found our way in the world as a new generation of religious leaders, we might freely tread in the footsteps of those who preceded us and leave our own imprints for those to come.

We simply could not get enough of Thurman. His wise teachings, his humility, his humor, were magnetic. Some of us, including myself, begged to stay in San Francisco with him. I remember that he thought our petitions to remain were so hilarious that he actually spat out his coffee, unable to refrain from his hearty laughter.[5] In his presence, as we were drawing near to the closing of our time together, I wrote the following lines, which illustrate the profound impact of his teaching on me as I struggled with the meaning and message of Jesus:

> dare we hear this?
>   no substitute?
>   no savior-man?
>   no god come twice?
>
> nothing but the integrity of my act?
>
> God has condemned me to freedom
>   I am a seed on the wind
>   landing somewhere
>   in strange territory
>   Is there a map?
>
> I was born naked
> I shall leave naked
> before God
> before humankind
> before me . . .
>
> God, this is a terrible joke
> this new insight
> this absurd revelation
> who will hear it?
> how shall I say it?
> who really wants freedom?
>
> the earth is the Lord's
> place my feet on the ground
> lead me home . . . 10/26/1979

For a new generation of leaders who seek a sense of wholeness in their personal and social struggles for "a friendly world under friendly skies,"[6] Thurman's wisdom and guidance for embarking on the inward journey is timely and crucial. In the following, we will look closely at the ways in which the inward journey can serve as a critical resource in the education and training of leaders who are spiritually disciplined, intellectually astute, and morally ANCHORED. We will proceed by mapping the inner landmarks of Thurman's core teachings, which include the meaning of the inward journey and the critical concepts and spiritual practices of knowledge of Presence, integrity, freedom, responsibility, love, and imagination that mark and arise from one's "fluid area of consent." I utilize Howard Thurman's life and work to map these six inner landmarks that leaders might employ as tools of the spirit. These tools may serve as disciplines and practices to sustain a sense of wholeness in the leader's private and public life.

THE INWARD JOURNEY

Howard Thurman's favorite collection of his meditations was *The Inward Journey.*[7] In many ways *The Inward Journey* captured for him what was at stake in the spiritual quest for wholeness, meaning, authenticity, and hope. It also served as a tutorial to the creative encounter where the seeker discovers *the fluid area of consent*—an interior space that makes available the resources to live *into* a life characterized by a sense of the vital that extends into the larger orbit of the social world and our struggles for justice. Having served as a teacher, pastor, and counselor to many leaders for over fifty-five years, Thurman insisted that they make an inward journey to the creative and precarious encounter with the Angel with the Flaming Sword. There, he argued, one discovers what is literal and irreducible in their being—an authentic and indivisible site of meaning and belonging. In various places, he called this moment "the creative encounter," "religious experience," "the sound of the genuine," "a sense of wholeness," or "yielding to the fluid area of one's consent." He writes in *The Inward Journey* that

> There is a sense of wholeness at the core of [humanity]
> That must abound in all [a person] does;
> That marks with reverence [a person's] ev'ry step;

That has its sway when all else fails;
That wearies out all evil things;
That warms the depth of frozen fears
Making friend of foe,
Making love of hate,
And lasts beyond the living and the dead,
Beyond the goals of peace, the ends of war!
This [person] seeks through all his [her] years:
To be complete and of one piece, within, without.[8]

INNER LANDMARKS

As a teacher and interpreter of religious experience, Thurman felt his primary role as a resource and guide so that the individual might find a place to choose where he or she would define and declare a sense of identity, purpose, and method.[9] He urged his readers and listeners to embark upon an inward journey—a voyage into the interior that brought them to "the conscious and direct exposure" with what they experienced as ultimate meaning. "Such an exposure" he added, "seems to the individual to be inclusive of all the meaning of life—there is nothing that is not involved."[10] The creative encounter is a cooperative affair or a "double search," where explorers on the inward journey discover that as they search, they are also being sought.[11] The experience is not casual; rather there is always a volitional element, an act of the will, involved. The self actively and consciously participates in the creative encounter;[12] and although the context of the experience may be casual or random, the individual must make a conscious decision to yield the fluid center of one's consent. This is part of an individual's freedom and serves as the ground for the moral quality of the will.[13]

KNOWLEDGE OF PRESENCE

The search for wholeness, integrity, and authenticity begins with knowledge of a sense of Presence. Thurman's formal understanding of *Presence* is indebted to his association with the Society of Friends' teachings on the Inner Light. This principle, sometimes referred to as the "seed," "the inner light," or "the root," maintains that within everyone there is an element of God, a divine intelligence and energy that discerns good and evil and opens the committed soul to the consciousness of its indwelling.[14]

Knowledge, therefore, does not refer only to ratiocination or the cognitive functions of the mind; rather it is a deep call to intimacy—to know and to be known. Thurman's favorite Scripture was Psalm 139, which speaks to this intimacy and the sense of Presence that "searches and knows" even as it is known. Thurman thought that this sense of Presence is at once an encounter with God and a revelation of one's sense of dignity and worth as child of God. He warns, however, that the journey to discovery is fraught with peril and hazard because knowledge requires death to innocence, a type of dismemberment or disintegration of that which is untested or unrealized. In other words, one does not merely *acquire* knowledge of self—it is *realized* through struggle, in the encounter with the Angel with the Flaming Sword. The Angel represents the utter trysting place of the encounter where innocence is shattered through the experience of *knowing*.[15] One discovers in the creative encounter the many identities and voices that have been mortgaged over the years in order to negotiate one's environment. But in the encounter these many selves that have been formed over a lifetime must give way, says Thurman, to that which is authentic and vital within the self. Critical for the encounter, therefore, is the agency or freedom of the individual who must re-member, retell, and relive the fragmented pieces of his or her defining narrative that are discovered in the Presence of God.[16] This space is a *fluid center* or *fluid area of consent*, a core of possibility, resilience, and resistance that will not yield even in the severest of circumstances, *le point le verge*.[17]

INTEGRITY

Closely related to Thurman's understanding of the knowledge of Presence is integrity. Integrity is the foundational principle upon which Thurman bases his understanding of the spiritual and moral life. While integrity encompasses truth-telling, sincerity, and honesty, attributes normally associated with good character and a virtuous life, for Thurman it is more. Integrity refers to integration, harmony, and wholeness in the personal life—in sum, it represents a sense of community within the person. He speaks of this idea in many places as *integrity* or *the integrity of the act*,[18] the place one calls one's own, and knowing one's name.

Thurman illustrates the significance of integrity as a spiritual practice in a sermon, titled "Who Are You?"[19] The sermon, based on the story of the Gerasene demoniac, speaks to Thurman's view that our personalities constitute a multiplicity of identities that compete for recognition, respect, and reverence from the other. In the traditional understanding of the story, the mad man was gripped by a demon, an unseen power that controlled and manipulated his behavior. Thurman says that when Jesus approached an ancient asylum where those so afflicted were exiled, this man ran out screaming. Jesus, sensing the man's problem, looked him in the eyes and asked the primary question of identity, "Who are you, really?" "What is your name?" According to Thurman, the man replied to Jesus' question, "You know, that's my whole problem. If I only knew my name . . . I am called 'Legion' because there are so many of us that we riot in the streets. If I only knew my name, this central truth of my existence, I would no longer act like a man without reason—but with purpose and depth."[20]

Naming and discovering one's identity and calling, for Thurman, is a dynamic and ongoing project of building a sense of wholeness and integration within. It begins first with the acknowledgment that there are within all of us many internalized others who are products of our constant negotiations with what he calls our "self-fact" and "self-image." Our self-fact, says Thurman, is our true identity as a child of God. Our self-image, on the other hand, is the product of our need to be seen by the other and to perform in certain behavioral patterns that are in conformity to the *look* of the other that is really a cry to be recognized, respected, and cared for. Ultimately, he thinks, we are unsuccessful because what we seek is already within us. Therefore, in vain we run "up and down the streets of other minds where no salutation greets and no place to call our own."[21]

In other words, Thurman suggests that the person who seeks a sense of identity and purpose must find a way, a spiritual practice, that allows the inner voices that are often in conflict to come together and cast a unanimous vote for the sake of wholeness, integration, and harmony within the self. Because *otherness* is so intricately bound to the formation of identity, Thurman felt it essential for leaders who are concerned about social justice and "the search for common ground" to begin within.[22] For leaders, especially those who have been historically marginalized, this is an invaluable tool of the spirit that allows them to respond from a fluid center that is not held hostage to the many socially constructed inner voices and identities that often prevent genuine acts of courage, justice, and compassion.

Finally, integrity is related to *commitment*. In his book *Disciplines of the Spirit*, Thurman identifies commitment as the initial spiritual discipline that calls one into the work of answering the questions of identity (Who am I?), purpose (What do I want?), and method (How do I propose to get it?).[23] Commitment, for Thurman, is more than mere intellectual assent or emotional attachment to an ideal, as in quest for social justice; rather, it is at the heart of one's personal religious experience, however defined. Commitment involves "singleness of mind": "This means surrendering the life at the very core of one's self-consciousness to a single end, goal, or purpose. When a man [woman] is able to bring to bear upon a single purpose all the powers of his [her] being, his [her] whole life is energized and vitalized."[24] This is particularly true, Thurman suggests, in the experience of crisis. In crisis, one is forced to ask the question of purpose, "What is it that I want, really?" He opines, "When a man [woman] faces this question put to him [her] by life, or when he [she] is caught up in the necessity of answering it, or by deliberate intent seeks an answer, he [she] is at once involved in the dynamics of commitment. At such a moment he [she] knows what, in the living of his [her] life, he [she] must be *for* and what he [she] must be *against*."[25]

LOVE

Thurman's understanding of love cannot be separated from his understanding of the knowledge of Presence and integrity. The knowledge of Presence—the deep intimacy of being known by God—is to experience the love of God, which affirms one's integrity and sense of self and relatedness to all of creation. A fundamental assumption in Thurman's thinking on the deep intimacy of interconnection between God and creation is what he calls "common consciousness," the affinity between human consciousness and other forms of sentient existence evident in nature. For Thurman, the theme of the kinship of all living things extends even into the realm of communication between animals, plants, and human beings. He reasons that if Life is one, then there ought to be a fundamental sense of unity at all levels of existence.

Therefore, for Thurman, love is not simply an interaction between human beings but is part of the very relationality of life and existence. As he wrote in *The Search for Common Ground,* "There seems to be a vast, almost incomprehensible interrelatedness tying all together. . . . [A person] is an organic part of the universe. In his [her] organism he experiences the order and harmony of the universe."[26] The existence of life for humans and other species is part of an unfolding interconnectedness. Thurman's understanding of love was grounded in his conviction that the harmony of the individual and the natural world are but separate aspects of a single phenomenon.

In a sermon titled "The Third Component" he illustrates this idea of "common consciousness." He tells a story from his youth when he rushed into his cousin's home and his cousin physically gestured for him not to move and to maintain quietness. To Thurman's surprise, the cousin pointed to his infant child playing with a rattlesnake in the backyard of the home. The child and the rattler, according to Thurman, were having a marvelous time at play. He suggested that this was a *for instance* of the ways in which "common consciousness" is present as something that is already given in our experience as creatures who are interrelated with other creatures—and by implication, it hearkens back to a sense of community that already exists in which we may participate with other forms of life in harmony, without threat.[27]

Common consciousness, then, is the unique, essential element that human beings share with all of life in its varied and manifold expressions of itself. For Thurman, it is the veritable creative presence of the Spirit of God that moves undisguised and uninhibited beneath all the complex and intricate stories that mark conscious existence, and yet it is the least observed and noted phenomenon of our existence. This living, pulsing, breathing dimension of experience, finds residence in human consciousness through cultivated disciplines that allow for the development of habits and practices that make the moral life possible.

Love is related to common consciousness as a *fundamentum* of existence, and it is in becoming aware our interrelatedness with all of creation that one experiences a sense of unity and wholeness in oneself and with the *other*—the other as person and other forms of creation. Thurman, therefore, defines love as "the experience through which a person passes when he [she] deals with another human being at a

point in that human being that is beyond all good and beyond all evil."
The experience of being loved "is the experience of being dealt with
at a point in oneself that is beyond all good and beyond all evil."[28]
Thurman believed that all love is of God, and therefore, to love is the
most profound act of life; only secondarily is loving an act of religion
or morality. Love is the fruit of the Presence of God; it is the power
that overcomes barriers that separate individuals, groups, and nations
from one another. Through the experience of love, one becomes aware
that he or she, however named or labeled by self or others, is completely understood, accepted, and free. For Thurman, this is the basis
of the moral life: to know that I am understood and accepted beyond
praiseworthiness and blame. For leaders, the sense of Presence, integrity, the abiding love and boundless understanding precipitates a radically new freedom, unmediated by the trappings of culture and societal
norms.

FREEDOM

As the grandson of a former slave who was raised in the segregated
South during the turn of the twentieth century, freedom was always at
the forefront of Howard Thurman's thinking. More than a quest for
citizenship rights or respect and recognition from the state, for Thurman freedom was a quest for personal assurance and security, which
are provided to the individual through the creative encounter. This
personal assurance and security is indispensable for leaders who struggle with racialized, sexualized and gendered identities,—or as James
Baldwin put it, ". . . this endless struggle to achieve and reveal and
confirm a human identity. . . ."[29] This struggle to achieve a sense of
self and identity, for Thurman, produces "a strange freedom" that is
in contradistinction to the authentic freedom that emerges and is nurtured by a sense of Presence, integrity, and love :

> It is a strange freedom to be adrift in the world of men [women]
> without a sense of anchor anywhere. . . . It is a strange freedom to go
> nameless up and down the streets of other minds where no salutation
> greets and no sign is given to mark the place one calls one's own. To
> be known, to be called by one's own name. . . . It is an honor to act
> as one's very own, it is to live a life that is one's very own, it is to bow

before an altar that is one's very own, it is to worship a God who is one's very own. It is a strange freedom to be adrift in the world of men [women], to act with no accounting, to go nameless up and down the streets of other minds where no salutation greets and no sign is given to mark the place one calls one's own.[30]

The strangeness of freedom and the sense of finding a place called one's own is rooted in *the hunger of the heart*—a yearning for a sense of authentic freedom, which is found in the creative encounter. Finding a place called *one's own* allows one to be at home in the midst of wind-tossed days and trying moments of self-examination. It is an anchor of the soul that holds fast in the turbulence of the shifting streams of personal and social struggles for justice.

Freedom, for Thurman, is first "the will and the ability to act at any moment in time as to influence or determine the future."[31] Implied in this view of freedom is the autonomy of the individual in the midst of social, physical and natural forces. Although the individual's destiny is to a large extent determined by these forces, ultimately one's sense of self cannot be defined by them. The second part of his definition of freedom sheds light on this important point. Freedom is "the sense of options or alternatives."[32] Freedom as a *sense of options* or alternatives is to be differentiated from freedom as an *exercise of options*. There are instances, says Thurman, when the exercise of options is impossible, that is, against natural, impersonal forces. Freedom as a sense of options or alternatives refers to the experience of the inner self located in the will, in the personal place where only the individual as individual can produce effect. He illustrates this view of freedom with a story from childhood in which he cornered a snake and placed his foot on it to hold it still. Even under the weight of his foot, Thurman said, he could still feel the small creature resisting by wiggling its tiny body. Thurman says that even though the snake could not escape, it kept alive a sense of options. This sense of options that the individual possesses as a part of her being is fundamental to freedom "and wherever this dies, wherever elements in the environment are internalized by people so as to paralyze this sense, then all the lights go out and the soul of the people begins to rot."[33] One thinks of great leaders like Martin Luther King Jr., Nelson Mandela, Rosa Parks, Fannie Lou Hamer, and Mahatma Gandhi who challenged the injustices of their times without yielding "the fluid area of their consent" by maintaining their sense of options. These exemplars of justice were able to engage in defiant acts of courage because they sustained a felt sense of options rooted in an integrated center that "like a tree planted by the waters, I shall not be moved."

Consequently, freedom is a quality of being; it is part of the "given-ness" of the individual as a child of God. To deny one's freedom, therefore, is to deny one's humanity. Thurman believed that freedom understood in this way enables leaders to experience a proper sense of self despite the ravages and insults heaped upon them by society and the world.

> "Freedom under God" means the recognition of the essential dig-nity of the human spirit; therefore it is inherent in man's [woman's] experience with life and is a basic ingredient in personality. This is so universal that it is the key to the intrinsic worthfulness which every man [woman] ascribes, at long last, to himself [herself]. There is a strange and mighty potency in the elemental knowledge that resides deep in the heart of every [person] that freedom under God is his [her] birthright as a child of God.[34]

RESPONSIBILITY

Freedom also entails responsibility.[35] The leader who is aware of her freedom is responsible not only for her *actions*, but for her *reactions* as well. Thurman suggests that responsibility is the corollary of freedom because when the individual assumes responsibility for her actions, she confirms the grounds of her own self and authenticity. Therefore, one can never unshoulder responsibility for one's actions and reactions without forfeiting one's own being.[36] This emphasis on responsibility has profound implications for the moral imperatives to practice love and integrity in *all* encounters and situations. For the oppressed, claim-ing responsibility for one's own destiny is the initial act of freedom and selfhood. Thurman writes, "If I let anyone take responsibility for my own actions, then I give them power of veto and certification over my life."[37]

The other side of responsibility is the leader's *reaction* to the events of her life. Thurman maintains that there is no escape or rationalization which releases us from the responsibility entailed in our free being. At all times, the individual maintains the right of veto and certification over how she responds to the circumstances of her life, even those that she cannot control.

> I can become a prisoner of events, I can cry aloud at the miscarriage of justice in the universe. I can do a whole range of things, but when I get through all my exhortations, my protestations, my agonizing, I am still left with the tight logic of my personal responsibility to say "yes" or "no" to my situation. Yes or no and make it stick. This is the freedom [a person] has. [One] does not have to say "yes" even to events he cannot control.[38]

Responsibility exists at both personal and social levels of existence. It is always a *shared* experience. The prerogative that the leader ascribes to herself must be carried over into relations with others. Hence, she is responsible as a member of the group and/or society in which she lives and functions. The privatization of responsibility is a denial of freedom. "Free men [women] must be responsible to themselves and to each other for the personal and collective life which marks their days."[39]

Finally, the ultimate responsibility is to God, the ground and guarantor of the individual's freedom. The leader who has yielded to "the fluid area of consent" is ultimately responsible to God for all *actions* and *reactions*. "God is the Creator of life," says Thurman, "and the ultimate responsibility of life is to God. [One's] responsibility to God is personal and solitary, but it is not experienced in isolation or detachment."[40] As societies participate in the dynamics and ends of life, they are also accountable to the God of life. Thurman argued that America as nation is morally responsible for its actions toward its citizens of color and the disinherited.[41]

In summary, the idea of freedom and the inherent responsibility for one's actions and reactions are key concepts in Thurman's view of the moral self and ethical theory. Innocence is given without knowledge; goodness, however, is achieved through knowledge and responsibility. For leaders, freedom and responsibility are practices that find their fulfillment in the personal encounter and knowing discovered in the Presence of God. Thurman felt strongly that meditation, prayer, and even suffering could become tools of the spirit that could bring one into this Presence. Freedom, therefore, is related to the practice of *knowing* as discussed earlier, because to become aware of one's freedom and responsibility to self, society, and God is to yield to one's "fluid area of consent" where one confronts the Angel with the Flaming Sword, which is our "crucial link with the Eternal."

> When the quality of goodness has been reestablished, a great change has taken place. Eyes are opened, knowledge is defined, and what results is the triumph of the quality of innocence over the quality of discord; a new synthesis is achieved that has in it the element of triumph. That is, a child is innocent, but a man [woman] who has learned how to winnow beauty out of ugliness, purity out of stain, tranquility out of tempest, joy out of sorrow, life out of death—only such a man [woman] may be said to be good. But he [she] is no longer innocent.[42]

IMAGINATION

A sixth tool of the spirit is the imagination. For Thurman, imagination is "the peculiar quality of mind that enables a man [woman] to stand in his [her] own place, defined by the uniqueness of his [her] life's story, and project himself [herself] into another person's life or situation. He [She] makes soundings there, looking out upon life through the other's eyes, even as he [she] remains himself [herself]. It is to inform one's self of the view from 'the other side.'"[43]

Imagination is a constituent part of the individual's nature as a self-transcendent being. Imagination becomes a veritable *angelos*, a messenger, when the individual through self-transcendence puts herself in another's place. Imagination, in this sense, is the agency through which empathy is realized and where one hears "the sound of the genuine" in one's self and in the other. Through imagination, the leader is enabled to transcend herself and reach others at the core of their being, at the seat of "common consciousness."[44] In doing so, the other is addressed at a place beyond all good and evil. This, according to Thurman, is the experience of love: when an individual is addressed at the centermost place of self, she experiences wholeness and harmony with the other and finds *common ground*: "I see you where you are, striving and struggling, and in the light of the highest possibility of your personality, I deal with you there."[45]

This usage of imagination, however, is neither "spiritualized" nor divorced from the exigencies of life and action. Rather for Thurman, it is a return to *the matter of matter* (to use Luther Smith's apt phrase-ology). Spirituality and social transformation are one fluid sentence in a larger narrative of the self in its quest for meaning and wholeness. This quest is rooted in the moral imagination, which creates the context for vigorous and creative public discourse where citizens hold one another accountable for what they know and value. It was with this sense of moral imagination that Thurman dared to experiment with ecclesial models at Howard University, the Church for the Fellowship of All Peoples in San Francisco, and Boston University. These ecclesial models held in bold relief a universal intent with broad appeal to interfaith worship and dialogue where dogma, creed, and theological perspectives found mutual concern with the transformation of society into a community.

GROUNDING QUESTIONS

1. List the six inner landmarks of the inward journey and ask yourself where you are at this moment on your leadership pilgrimage. What are the specific challenges and opportunities that present themselves at each landmark for the fulfillment of your leadership goals and objectives?
2. In our deepest and most intimate encounters with the Presence, as you exercise your *fluid area of consent*, what are the many voices that compete to be heard?
3. How are the voices competing for your attention related to your calling and vocation? Which voices shall you allow the Angel to sever, and which voices will you re-member in your quest for a sense of wholeness and integrity?
4. How do you begin to rename and re-language your sense of calling and vocation, beginning with your own sense of self and place?
5. Identify leaders who have exhibited freedom as a sense of options that helped them to lead with a sense of Presence, integrity, love, responsibility, and imagination. Mind that these leaders need not be well-known. What inner landmarks in these leaders most appeal to you?
6. Are there lessons from other leaders that you can apply in your own quest for courage, justice, and compassion by maintaining freedom as a sense of options?

7. To whom and what are you ultimately accountable? Before you answer this question, make a list beginning with the orbit of personal and social obligations that you experience in your intimate settings and in your professional or vocational relationships. How do these obligations relate to your ultimate responsibility to God and your immediate community?

4

Thurman-eutics

Howard Thurman's "Clothesline" for the Interpretation of the Life of the Mind and Journey of the Spirit

SHIVELY T. J. SMITH

". . . one may find it extremely helpful to discover a clothesline" on which all of one's feelings and thoughts and desires may be placed. It may be a simple sentence like the great organ note with which the 139th Psalm opens, "O Lord, thou hast searched me, and known me. Thou knowest my downsitting and mine uprising, thou understandest my thought afar off." Or it may be some long forgotten but now subtly recalled line from a hymn or a phrase from a prayer heard at another period. . . . Often the focusing of the mind upon some phase of the life of the Master will fill the whole being with irradiation, and one finds one's way to the very presence of God.

When one has thus prepared, a strange thing happens. It is very difficult to put into words. The initiative slips out of one's hands and into the hands of God. . . .

—Howard Thurman, *The Creative Encounter*[1]

INTRODUCTION

Whenever I contemplate Thurman's clothesline, I find myself reminiscing about my childhood. I remember summer vacations at my grandparents' white-shingled house in Winchester, Kentucky. The smells of homemade yeast rolls fresh out of the oven, roasting fresh vegetables from the garden, lemon fresh cleaner wafting through my grandmother's pristinely kept living room—these memories are precious and sweet. Recollections filled with the sounds of laughter and chatter rising from the inner parlor where my great aunts and uncles sat swapping stories from the "old days" lift my spirits *these* days. Some reminiscences of my childhood carry me through my life's journeys and adventures, but perhaps none are so deeply imprinted in my inner mind as my grandparent's backyard.

Soon after I arrived at my grandparents' house, I often ran to the backyard to see if the clotheslines were strung from the back porch and running down the hill to the old wooden shed sitting at the edge of the property line. Sometimes my grandmother strung six and seven lines of heavy twine up and down the backyard. My grandfather erected wooden stakes from the ground and attached them to the lines to support the weight of the laundry. Those wooden poles made the lines sturdy, stable, and resistant to the breeze. They were even resilient against tenacious and playful grandchildren who deemed the rows of clotheslines draped in laundry conducive to playing hide-and-seek or any number of other imagined escapades.

With natural gusts blowing through them, the laundry, especially the rows of white bed linens, would make such beautiful, flowing silhouettes and flapping melodies of wind and fabric. The smell of fresh linens, mixed with my grandmother's sweet scent, drifted toward me every time I stood among them in the breeze. As a child, I imagined angels hiding among those sheets. My young mind reasoned that no one else but angels could make those rippling sounds and calming, refreshing aromas.

I watched those linens wafting in the wind with recognition that as much as they were free, they were also held in place by wooden clothespins. Those linens were beautiful because they were both free and ANCHORED. Whenever I had a chance, I grabbed a book and sat among the clotheslines to read, write, dream, pretend, and even talk to God and my ancestors. There was something safe and open about sitting on the grass amid that which represented what was unrestricted yet anchored, drifting yet bound, rippling in the breeze yet serene and holy. My grandmother's clothesline was a simple, mundane human instrument used for matters of hygiene and dress. Yet, it represented a paradoxical blend of liberation and fixity that has held me steady in the most devastating windstorms.

In my first reading of Howard Thurman's book *The Creative Encounter*, I paused at the passage above about the discovery of "a clothesline." Thurman casts the clothesline as the place where all our feelings, thoughts, and desires can hang suspended by the initiatives of not just ourselves but by the initiatives of a Divine Presence, God, who is greater than us. Living in societies that tout mantras like "I am the captain of my fate" or "I am the controller of my own success," we may find ourselves both humbled and emboldened by the reminder that there is a greater force animating our existence. It carries the cautionary tone of the biblical saying, "I say to everyone among you not to think of yourself more highly than you ought to think" (Rom. 12:3), reminding us that we are members of humanity and participants in God's creation, rather than lords over it. Thurman's image of a clothesline can also birth a newfound, childlike wonder in us for what is possible and not yet.

Since my early twenties and undergraduate studies in religion and philosophy, I have found Thurman's clothesline image an affirmation that my intellectual and spiritual selves are not in opposition. Education and spirituality can work hand-in-hand even when the realities and expectations of adulthood, academia, religious affiliation, citizenship, and social etiquette (to name a few) may say otherwise. To engage the clothesline of initiatives active in our living is to understand that the mechanisms of the mind and spirit work in tandem in our spiritual journeying, intellectual undertakings, and daily practices of interpreting the world around us. As Thurman says, "For every man [woman] there is a necessity to establish as securely as possible the lines along which [s]he proposes to live his [her] life."[2]

In this chapter, I explore Thurman's writings and ideas about the mystical relationship between head, heart, and lived experience from the vantage of an African American woman raised in the South, who was born on the cusp between Generation X and the Millennial generation. I am a professor of biblical history and interpretation. I hold this role with pride and malcontent, as I am the first in my family to earn a doctorate. I, too, am a child of the church, who was raised as a pastor's kid and later ordained as clergy in the African Methodist Episcopal Church. I am a lifelong learner who found her voice through reading, writing, and leaving the nest to launch into the unknown world. Howard Thurman has been my faithful travel companion.

For me, Thurman's clothesline is not simply a strategy for an individualistic spirituality, disengaged from and unaccountable to the realities and hardships of daily living. According to Thurman, to be a mystic or one devoted to the life of the inner person is to also be committed to life-giving human relations and equitable societies in which one's mind, spirit, and personality dwell. The image of the clothesline, briefly presented by Thurman, can support our endeavors to chart pathways for wholeness, kinship, and flourishing. It can awaken us to the mystical dance between our minds and spirits as we live in and make sense of a world struggling to make its paths straight, just, and affirming for all. This is *my* journey through Thurman's head, heart, and practice of interpretation.[3]

THURMAN'S VISUAL LANDSCAPE:
IMAGES OF THE INNER WORLD,
PICTURES OF DIVINE PRESENCE

Thurman's writings are a rich and stimulating repository of images that derive from his life. They are intended to move us toward new dreams and rouse awareness of our inner and outer visual landscapes. His images point us toward realities beyond what is familiar. In *Meditations of the Heart*, Thurman inspires us by saying,

> As long as a man [woman] has a dream in his [her] heart, [s]he cannot lose the significance of living. . . . The dream in the heart is the outlet. It is the one with the living water welling up from the very springs of Being, nourishing and sustaining all of life. Where there is no dream, the life becomes a swamp, a dreary dead place and, deep within, a man's [woman's] heart begins to rot. The dream need not be some great and overwhelming plan; it need not be a dramatic picture of what might or must be someday; it need not be a concrete outpouring of world-shaking possibility of sure fulfillment. . . .
>
> The dream is the quiet persistence in the heart that enables a man [woman] to ride out the storms of his [her] churning experiences. It is the exciting whisper moving through the aisles of his [her] spirit answering the monotony of limitless days of dull routine. It is the ever-recurring melody in the midst of the broken harmony and harsh discords of human conflict. It is the touch of significance, which highlights the ordinary experience, the common event. The dream is no outward thing. It does not take its rise from the environment in which one moves or functions. It lives in the inward parts, it is deep within, where the issues of life and death are ultimately determined. Keep alive the dream; for as long as a man [woman] has a dream in his [her] heart, [s]he cannot lose the significance of living.[4]

In this extended passage alone, images such as water channel outlets, wellsprings, swamps, stormy weather, music, and church aisles and pews convey the vision Thurman is casting for his readers. Thurman's writings and speeches stimulate spiritual and intellectual reconfiguration by appealing to what one knows, feels, perceives, and desires. The development of one's inner person is not wholly disembodied and abstract. That is not the mystical life that Thurman advances.

To this end, Thurman's selection of images was not arbitrary, but intentionally chosen to re-form his hearers and readers in their inner processes and outward relations with God and other human beings, near and abroad. At all times, Thurman lived engaged in an experiment of tilling the inward person's mind and heart to heighten awareness and prepare her for possible encounters with the Divine Presence, other human beings, and creation. The mystical life foments religious experience that matures both intrapersonal intelligence and interpersonal relations:

> The central fact in religious experience is the awareness of meeting God. The descriptive words used are varied: sometimes it is called an encounter; sometimes, a confrontation; and sometimes, a sense of Presence. What is insisted upon, however, without regard to the term used, is that in the experience defined as religious, the individual is seen as being exposed to direct knowledge of ultimate meaning, *ne plus ultra* being, in which all that the individual is, becomes clear as immediate and often distinct revelation. [S]he is face to face with something which is so much more, and so much more inclusive, than all of his [her] awareness of himself [herself] that for him [her], in the moment, there are no questions. Without asking, somehow [s]he knows.[5]

Not only did Thurman's images reflect the world, they also sparked the spiritual and mental imaginations of his hearers and readers so we could envision new worlds defined by new configurations in human kinship, fellowship, and community. Thurman's imagery is so vibrant and potent it is hard to look away and even harder to forget because it is penned to open us up to Presence, rather than to close us off from it.

Indeed, there is something very concrete in Thurman's teaching about the mind and spirit of the inner person. Using word pictures, he articulates "the anatomy of the relationship between" different people groups—especially the powerful and the powerless, the dominating and the dominated—against a larger world background of colonization, slavery, systemic disenfranchisement, and poverty of diverse masses. As a member of the Black community in America, born on November 18, 1899, just a few decades after the abolition of slavery, Thurman does not attempt to escape nor diminish the spiritual and psychological plight of his own people. Rather, he leverages that social and spiritual history in his own seeking of the head and heart of others in the world. To engage Thurman's God-talk and to consider what is the source and substance of our religious experiences as intellectual and spiritual beings involves not only revisiting the mundane visuals of Thurman's childhood and life but also accepting his invitation to revisit our own.

THURMAN-EUTICS INTRODUCED:
UNHINGING HERMENEUTICS TO GROW
IN AWARENESS OF GOD AND NEIGHBOR

Thurman's image of the clothesline, informed by my grandmother's clothesline, is a generative way forward in considering the human pursuit for knowledge and spiritual meaning. Though sparsely used, the importance of "the clothesline" metaphor to Thurman's thinking, particularly his interpretations of the mundane details of life and our spiritual journey among them, can be easily overlooked. Such oversight is a grave loss because Thurman's clothesline image carries within it the markers of his interpretative practice and lens. This is what scholars of theology and philosophy call "hermeneutics."[6]

For Thurman, hermeneutics—the practice of articulating *how* humans interpret—grows out of the relational self that is seeking to experience God in all people, places, and things. The seeking spirit and the seeking mind are not unhinged, randomly skipping from one object of study to another. Thurman's image of the clothesline, "on which all of one's feelings and thoughts and desires may be placed," suggests that even the most liberated mind and spirit is tied to something. It is linked to a potentially temporal "knowing," which can give way to another "knowing." In his book *Deep Is the Hunger*, Thurman says, "Not only is faith a way of knowing, a form of knowledge, but it is also one of life's great teachers. At no point is this fact more clearly demonstrated than in an individual's growing knowledge of God."[7] The purpose of our interpretative practices, according to Thurman, is not just to arrive at more insights that are impressive and emotive; the aim of conscious interpretative practice is to grow in awareness of God's presence, even as full knowledge of God always evades us. "Thurman-eutics," therefore, is about the humble, yet persistent, pursuit for understanding that Thurman deems necessary for whole living, though the journey to wholeness is never complete.

A unique idea about the human practice of interpretation runs throughout Thurman's writings, sermons, and speeches. Thurman argues repeatedly that all of life, society, cultural norms, and the created world are our interpretative mechanisms for accessing and encountering God. He says, "Religious experience is interpreted to mean the conscious and direct exposure of the individual to God. Such an experience seems to the individual to be inclusive of all the meaning of his [her] life—there is nothing that is not involved."[8] At all times, for Thurman, the knowledge of God grows as genuine recognition of the "other" grows. In Thurman-eutics, the interpretative voice is a by-product of our own disciplined sensitivity and responsiveness to the opportunities around us for new encounters with God and a growing sympathetic familiarity with people we meet. One begins with "self as text" because it is the most present and most accessible first site of an encounter with God. Thurman says, "In religious experience God meets the individual at the level not only of the individual's needs, but also, in my judgment more incisively, at the level of his [her] residue of God-meaning and goes forward from there."[9]

Thurman believed in the common journey shared between the life of the mind and the life of the spirit. His descriptions carry within them the list of resources at the disposal of one who consciously takes on the endeavor to journey in her mind and spirit toward something that will always escape her grasp. Feelings, thoughts, desires, and initiatives interacting with broader spiritual and social awareness—these are matters of head and heart, as Thurman's autobiography narrates. Thus, Thurman-eutics is a deep orientation toward relationship, proximity, and synthesis. It is the practice of experiencing and talking about God from a place of connection to not just what is "other" and unattainable but also from places of familiarity and the processes of living itself.

EMBODIED MEANING-MAKING:
THE LIFE OF THE MIND
AND THE JOURNEY OF THE SPIRIT AS ONE

Thurman spent much of his time in the work of *interpretation*, wresting meaning from the world and his experience of it. For Thurman, to make meaning of the self, of texts (sacred or ordinary), of the societies we live in, and of God is to be wholly *embodied*. To arrive at a careful and informed understanding of what a text means—lived or literary in nature—is to utilize the resources of all our living, not just the mind part of our being nor the spirit. It is to use all of it.

Growing up, and especially when I started college, the life of the mind and the journey of the spirit were out of sync "dance partners"; they struggled to move within me in unison. I dared not bring the rhythms of my spirit into the ivory halls of academia or the critical nimbleness of my mind inside the faith-filled walls of church. It was as though I was keeping each a secret from the other. A divided life, I lived—until I realized Thurman bore this secret, too.

> In the total religious experience, we learn how to wait; we learn how to ready the mind and the spirit. It is in the waiting, brooding, lingering, tarrying timeless moments that the essence of the religious experience becomes most fruitful. . . . I work at preparing my mind, my spirit for the moment when God comes to Himself [Herself] in me. When it happens, I experience His [Her]Presence. When this experience becomes an object of thought and reflection, it is then that my mind creates dogmas, creeds and doctrines. These are the creations of the mind and are therefore always after the fact of the religious experience. But they are always out of date. The religious experience is always current, always fresh.[10]

Mind and spirit, head and heart—they are not separate entities working against each other in the writings of Thurman. Rather, Thurman assumes they work together toward religious experiences that awaken us to worlds we may live in and nevertheless fail to comprehend. Thurman's writings invite those of us committed to a life of learning to also be devoted to a life of the spirit that informs, shapes, and irradiates our greatest intellectual endeavors. He writes about head and heart together to express the essential connection they can nurture in us to transgress our self-imposed boundaries, be it intentional or not, and to embrace the reshaping that can occur by engaging other peoples, histories, ideas, and experiences with the totality of our living and location in the world.

Thurman's clothesline imagery suggests we make sense of our feelings, thoughts, and desires by leveraging the twine of interwoven initiatives they hang upon. The clothesline is not just an image but also an interpretative key for how to make life-giving meaning in our pursuits for the life of the mind and the journey of the spirit. We use the spiritual resources of our hearts and the recollections of our minds to understand ourselves and the worlds around us, seen and unseen. Thurman says it best:

There must be a *will* to understand which informs the integrity of one's desire to understand. How much "more true" is it in the understanding of ideas, of experiences, yes, of the complexities of human beings. It takes time and effort and imagination. It does not come merely for the asking. One has to "fool around" the edges of another's life, getting closer and closer to the central place. . . . The basis of one's strength in understanding, is the vast and unlimited understanding of God, who is the source and ground of all being.[11]

INTERPRETING JESUS THROUGH
THE EYES OF HOWARD THURMAN

In addition to treating the life of the mind and the journey of the spirit as joint endeavors in religious experience, Thurman pins much of his teachings and ponderings about the inner person, mystical life, and human fellowship to the clothesline of a historic, religious figure: Jesus. *How* Thurman interprets Jesus is essential to understanding his probing conversations about the life of the mystic and her social presence, the life of the inner person connected to her material context, and the life of an individual located among the diverse peoples of the world. He interprets the story and substance of Jesus in a variety of ways and to a variety of ends, all of which are distinct from meanings enunciated by mainstream American Christianity of the early and mid-twentieth century.

Sociohistorical Context of Jesus
through Thurman's Interpretive Lens

Growing up in the Black community of Daytona Beach, Florida, under the nurturing care of his mother and grandmother, freedwomen and devoted Christians, Thurman's Black Christian roots were unshakable. Thurman was clear that his understanding of Christianity was not akin to its manifestations as practiced by much of white American Christianity. Indeed, Thurman had many critiques about Western forms of Christianity that interpreted Jesus and the gospel as an affirmation of dominance and privilege rather than a critique of violent separateness and acts of power over others. To this end, Thurman identifies two broad strategies for reading the figure of Jesus. He said, "It is a privilege, after so long a time, to set down what seems to me to be an essentially creative and prognostic interpretation of Jesus as religious subject rather than religious object."[12] According to Thurman, Jesus could be interpreted as either the subject or object of religious experience and meaning.

Thurman suggests focusing on Jesus as a religious object, abstracts him from the original sociohistorical situation in which he was born and to which he responded. As such, he becomes an easily co-opted image that can and has been weaponized as an instrument for destroying life, dispossessing people of their identities, destroying the communities of outsiders, and ultimately exacting death on those not a part of the dominant powerful class. In Thurman's estimation, white American Christianity—especially slaveholding and Jim Crow observant Christianity—distorted the religious and social values Jesus espoused and embodied by wielding him as an object of religion detached from actual historical, political, and religious situations.

Thurman asserted that the proper understanding of Jesus' life and commitments should raise awareness of how current national and international mutations of white Christianity were inimical to the gospel ethic of love and equitable human relations. Thurman's unique interpretative approach to Jesus is grounded in his perspective of Jesus' value to the religious life and confession of the poor, exploited, persecuted, and dispossessed in American Christian society as well as colonized societies abroad.

Thurman understood Jesus as the prophetic Savior who was *one of* the disinherited, not just *one commissioned to go* to them. This is the understanding of Jesus that Thurman championed by repositioning interpretations of Jesus in the Christian faith that privilege the experience and struggles of the disinherited without erasing the humanity of dominant groups. Consequently, the interpretative key for understanding Jesus as the Christ in Christianity, for Thurman, is in viewing him as a religious subject born in and shaped by communities living on the underside of imperial power and domination.

For Thurman, understanding Jesus requires reckoning with his identity as a divine prophet and Savior in conversation with "the fact" of his social realities and status as well as his personality. "It is necessary to examine the religion of Jesus against the background of his own age and people, and to inquire into the content of his teaching with reference to the disinherited and the underprivileged."[13]

Jesus's location as a Jew, living under the regime of the Roman Empire in Palestine in the first century CE, was not the only historical fact upon which Thurman hung his interpretative engagement.

Thurman also acknowledged that Jesus was a poor Jew. For Thurman, Jesus was from a people and community with cultural histories, traditions, beliefs, stories, and commitments who were colonized with many living in poverty, struggling from the edges of societal resources and access. This is the Jesus-subject Thurman interprets.

Three Interpretations of Jesus as One in Mind and Spirit

Thurman's particular interpretation of Jesus or hermeneutical approach to appropriating the meaning of Jesus for Christian belief and religious experience, broadly construed, appears throughout his writings. Chief among these writings is *Jesus and the Disinherited*, which reflects at least three approaches to interpreting the import of Jesus for the mystical life of the mind and spirit. Thurman interprets Jesus (1) for his religion in context (what he believed in convictions), (2) for his teaching in context (what he provided as instruction), and (3) for his model in context (what he did in practice).

First, Thurman interpreted Jesus for his religion in context. As noted above, the religion of Jesus cannot be separated from his identity as a Jew living as a non-citizen under Roman imperial power. It is the claim to citizenship and access that distinguishes the usefulness of Paul's writings and concepts from Jesus. Whereas Paul could and did claim his Roman citizenship when necessary, according to Thurman, Jesus' combined religious and ethnic identity did not offer such a luxury.

> Now Jesus was not a Roman citizen. He was not protected by the normal guarantees of citizenship—that quiet sense of security which comes from knowing that you belong and the general climate of confidence which it inspires. If a Roman soldier pushed Jesus into a ditch, he could not appeal to Caesar; he would be just another Jew in the ditch. Standing always beyond the reach of citizen security, he was perpetually exposed to all the "arrow of outrageous fortune," and there was only a gratuitous refuge—if any—within the state. What stark insecurity! What a breeder of complete civil and moral nihilism and psychic anarchy! Unless one actually lives day by day without a sense of security, he [she] cannot understand what worlds separated Jesus from Paul.[14]

Second, Thurman interpreted Jesus for his teaching in context. Thurman probed the stories of Jesus engrossed in the question, "Is there any help to be found for the disinherited in the religion of Jesus?"[15] For Thurman, the clothesline of Jesus' teaching is the context from which the instruction emerged. In other words, what Jesus said to do cannot be abstracted from *where* in the social world Jesus made these assertions—namely, from the place of the disenfranchised, marginal, and non-citizen of the Roman world.

Thurman asserted the religion of Jesus did not view the violent, exclusionary tactics of the current world order as a generative environment conducive for nurturing whole, anchored, and affirmed lives. The religion of Jesus, according to Thurman, was characterized by a belief that everyone is God's people and it affirmed no person should be a threat to their sisters and brothers. Moreover, the religion of Jesus, born out of a Roman imperial context, taught the necessity of making room so all humanity and creation could be included and secure.[16] In this way, Thurman employed the muscles of mind and spirit to make theological and anthropological statements as well as ecological assertions.

Third, Thurman interprets Jesus for his model of how to live a religiously inspired public life in a world dominated by human powers and institutions, which deem legal the systemic marginalizing, violence, abuse, erasure, and annihilation of individuals and their communities. He says, ". . . the striking similarity between the social position of Jesus in Palestine and that of the vast majority of American Negroes is obvious to anyone who tarries long over the facts. We are dealing here with conditions that produce essentially the same psychology."[17] From Thurman's location as a Black Christian male raised in the segregated South and navigating the racist systems of the North, Jesus' contextual practices provide resources for the spiritual and mental life of the oppressed. It is the earthly, historical person of Jesus—not simply in his identity as the Christ or Son of God—but in his doing as a commissioned human agent of God that captivated Thurman and guided his spiritual practices and mental dispositions.

Thurman saw in the religious practices modeled by Jesus, and other spiritual leaders like Mahatma Gandhi, a "spiritually based social struggle" that provided resources to the sociopolitical predicaments of African Americans and all colonized peoples who have historically suffered under the hegemonic regimes of the white, Western world.[18] Hence, Thurman interprets Jesus as a model for what to do as communities called to religiously inspired and prophetic public agency when those same communities are in need of ". . . profound succor and strength to enable them to live in the present with dignity and creativity."[19]

CONCLUSIONS

The creative encounter is the life of the mind and the spirit meeting God and navigating human life and relations. Thurman's clothes-line illuminates how the practice of interpretation functions to unite us to Presence, divine and human. At the heart of what I refer to as "Thurman-eutics," is Thurman's practice of interpreting the texts of the world—literary and lived, semantic and visual, sacred and ordinary—for the cultivation of the inner person and the facts of human context. Interpretation and the mystical life is not an avenue for escaping the injustices, difficulties, and suffering as well as the luxuries and comforts of our material world. It is not a mechanism for retreating into our inward center unaccountable to the realities of our context.

Thurman's clothesline ties the most authentic part of our being—our feelings, our thoughts, our desires, and the ways we make sense of the world and ourselves—to God, whom we can never fully interpret and understand. Yet, many of us, using our heads and hearts, join Thurman in a search for God in the daily rhythms of life that are exceptional and common, extraordinary and mundane, real and imagined. A few days ago, while reading Thurman's prose, I remembered how the summer breeze wafted through my grandmother's clothespinned sheets. Immediately, I was reminded that God's clothesline is strong enough to support the workings of my mind and journeying of my spirit. For as Thurman-eutics uncovers, they are One.

GROUNDING QUESTIONS

1. What are images or items from your childhood that are not immediately "religious" in nature though they carry spiritual meaning for you?
2. What are examples from your living experience when the life of the mind and journey of the spirit have been divided and when they have shared the same path?
3. What values constitute your clothesline of interpretation upon which hangs your feelings, desires, beliefs, and initiatives?

PART 3

Thurman as Anchor for Activists

Interlude

Emergence Within

STEPHEN LEWIS

As the sun's rising countenance pierced between breaks in the forest's canopy, I made my way down the dimly lit path to the river's edge. The hovering fog from nightfall blanketed the coursing current between the river's banks. The rhythm of time slowed to a snail's pace. The river whistled onward. And, there I stood meditatively, staring into the shimmering daylight reflecting against the luminous, dark, translucent surface of the river. Transfixed, I watch the currents colliding, absorbing, and creating with one another different patterns as they journeyed downstream.

Then, emergence appeared. Another world, the otherworld, broke the visible plane. Suddenly, I was offered a glimpse of, if not an encounter with, me. As quickly as it came the otherworld disappeared into the sublime reality of the unknown.

Eyes wide open, I stood startled, shocked, and awed. What broke my concentration, my meditation, my mystical encounter with self? Was it the fight or flight adrenaline coursing through my veins? In wonderment, goose bumps populated up and down my arms like an allergic reaction; a bodily response to my encounter with the sacred, the Holy.

Was this otherworldly encounter a coincidence? Or was this a serendipitous moment. Either way, I was entranced by:

> Emergence.
> From below,
> within,
> a world unbeknownst to me
> awakened a profound awareness
> that lay dormant,
> within me.

Beneath the surface
emergence withdrew.
Instincts invited me to pursue,
and plunge beneath the surface
to discover a world I never knew;
home.

In the depths of stillness, I intuited a response to my unspoken question—what does the Eternal long for me to know about the unfolding nature of vocation, specifically my vocational journey?

Nature is speaking to you.
A world you cannot fully comprehend.
Explore what's beneath the surface in you,
beyond you, deep within you,
the world that inhabits you,
speaks to you, and longs to commune with you.

An otherworld
governed by
a different set of rules,
laws and circumstances
beyond, between, and among
your rational world.

Emergence.
Do the reversal,
emerge within.
And stay
for a while.

As I ascended from the shoreside classroom, the river continued to teach. Nature is speaking, singing, and reminding us: God is within me, within you. But to heed these lessons, are we listening and tuning into Wisdom's frequency? What might we create together if we did tune into each other? How might our nature and shared frequency draw out our potential and lead us to encounter the Emergence within?

5

Prophetic Service and Global Change

MARIAN WRIGHT EDELMAN

A LITANY OF THANKSGIVING

Today, I make my Sacrament of Thanksgiving.

I begin with the simple things of my days:
    Fresh air to breathe,
    Cool water to drink,
    The taste of food,
    The protection of houses and clothes,
    The comforts of home.
For these, I make an act of Thanksgiving this day!

I bring to mind all the warmth of humankind that I have known:
    My mother's arms,
    The strength of my father,
    The playmates of my childhood,
    The wonderful stories brought to me from the lives of many who
        talked of days gone by when fairies and giants and all kinds of
        magic held sway;
    The tears I have shed, the tears I have seen;
    The excitement of laughter and the twinkle in the eye with its
        reminder that life is good.
For all these I make an act of Thanksgiving this day.

I finger one by one the messages of hope that awaited me at the
crossroads:
> The smile of approval from those who held in their hands the reins
> of my security;
> The tightening of the grip in a single handshake when I feared the
> step before me in the darkness,
> The whisper in my heart when the temptation was fiercest and the
> claims of appetite were not to be denied,
> The crucial word said, the simple sentence from an open page
> when my decision hung in the balance.

For all these I make an act of Thanksgiving this day.

I pass before us the mainsprings of my heritage:
> The fruits of the labors of countless generations who lived before
> me, without whom my own life would have no meaning;
> The seers who saw visions and dreamed dreams;
> The prophets who sensed a truth greater than the mind could
> grasp and whose words could only find fulfillment in the years
> which they would never see,
> The workers whose sweat has watered the trees, the leaves of which
> are for the healing of the nations;
> The pilgrims who set their sails for lands beyond all horizons,
> whose courage made paths into new worlds and far-off
> places;
> The saviors whose blood was shed with the recklessness that
> only a dream could inspire and God could command.

For all these I make an act of Thanksgiving this day.

I linger over the meaning of my own life and the commitment to
which I give the loyalty of my heart and mind:
> The little purposes in which I have shared with my loves, my
> desires, my gifts;
> The restlessness which bottoms all I do with its stark insistence
> that I have never done my best, I have never dared to reach for
> the highest;
> The big hope that never quite deserts me, that I and my kind will
> study war no more, that love and tenderness and all the inner
> graces of Almighty affection will cover the life of the children of
> God as the waters cover the sea.

All these and more than mind can think and heart can feel,
I make as my sacrament of Thanksgiving to Thee,
Our Father, in humbleness of mind and simplicity of heart.[1]

STANDING WITH THOSE WHOSE BACKS ARE AGAINST THE WALL: PULLING THE THREAD

Howard Thurman and I were both born in the segregated South—he in Daytona Beach, Florida, in 1899, I in Bennettsville, South Carolina, in 1939. The segregation of those times and places was blatantly racist, unjust, and grated on the spirit.

Black children had worse schools and more limited educational opportunities than white children. Thurman had to go to Jacksonville for high school because of Daytona Beach's dearth of educational options at the time. I graduated from an all-Black high school about two years after *Brown v. Board of Education*, a school that had been hastily built trying to project an image of "equal" from the outside before *Brown* was decided, but remained inferior on the inside with outdated equipment and hand-me-down books that more truly reflected the school district's failure to value Black and white children equally.

The wealth of literature housed in our towns' libraries were reserved for whites alone during my childhood. That exclusion didn't stop us. My parents always had books in our homes. They were more important than a second pair of shoes. I would lose myself with books in my minister father's book-lined study. Both he and my mother considered books necessities, not luxuries, and a variety of magazines like the *Christian Century* and a range of newspapers kept us abreast of happenings around the world and in the Black community. As an adult, I was honored by my hometown's building of a new public library renamed for me. I was pleased with the inscription carved in stone over the doorway: "All Are Welcome." It is a very attractive hub of community life. As a student at Morehouse College, Thurman is said to have devoured every volume its library held.[2]

Hardworking Black parents struggled to bring home paychecks to provide for their families. Thurman was raised by his grandmother, Nancy, who had been born into slavery, and his family experienced the financial difficulties of so many Black families in that era. Likewise, my parents never hesitated to open our home and add a place at our table for those in our community who were struggling, but who shared generously with their pastor from their gardens and canned foods. Still, there were children in our town who died because of poverty, lack of health care, or as a result of racism. A lifetime later I still remember little Johnny Harrington, who stepped on a nail and didn't get a shot and died of tetanus. I recall vividly the migrant family that had a car collision with a truck driven by whites and an ambulance driver who refused to take them to the hospital because they were Black.

Despite this broader context of segregation, racism, and limited public educational and financial opportunities, both Howard Thurman and I had rich childhoods, thanks to our families of deep faith. I was extremely lucky to have parents who had been college educated and exposed us to great role models. Of Thurman's childhood, Walter Fluker wrote,

> Finding in the fold of his neighborhood and in nature his "windbreak against existence," Thurman showed early signs of mystical engagement with the world for which he would later become famous. Reared by his beloved Grandma Nancy, a former slave, young Thurman regularly read the Bible aloud to her as a child. From her he learned not only of the trials of slavery, but also of the slaves' deep religious faith, which profoundly shaped his later vision of the transformative promise of African American Christianity.[3]

My parents and other elders in my childhood likewise created a bulwark and buffer from the segregated and hostile world that told us we weren't important. As I reflected in *Guide My Feet: Prayers and Meditations on Loving and Working for Children,*

> After many challenges and successes in . . . decades of service to children, again and again I have drawn on my childhood experiences when family, church, the extended community family, and teachers provided a seamless web of support for Black children. Although stigmatized and devalued by the external world in an era of racial apartheid, when government not only did not help but hindered, Black adults refused to let external barriers become internal ones. They wrapped children in a cocoon of caring and activity. And they knew that the care of the mind and body needed to be grounded in the care of the spirit, which was the glue that held our families and our community together.[4]

Given the love, faith, and support of our families and community elders, no wonder that what came to Thurman's lips and mine is not bitterness or diatribe but thanksgiving, a thanksgiving that starts with gratitude for the simple comforts of home, our mothers' arms and the strength of our fathers, and culminates in a sense of purpose, calling, and commitment to a life of meaning and service.

While more than a century has passed since Thurman's childhood, and nearly three-quarters since my own, millions of children still "stand, at a moment in human history, with their backs against the wall," to use Thurman's unforgettable phrase in *Jesus and the Disinherited*.[5] Children of color, children in poverty, children of immigrants, LGBTQ children, children in the cradle to prison pipeline, and so many others—are still growing up in a society that is racist, unjust, violent, and unwelcoming for millions of children. While legal segregation has ended, most Black, brown, and impoverished students still attend de facto segregated schools, many with decrepit buildings, disgracefully limited resources, zero-tolerance school discipline policies that criminalize minor and nonviolent childhood infractions and misbehavior, low expectations, and dismal graduation rates. Hardworking parents, with their backs against the wall, still struggle to earn a living wage and to afford nutritious food, safe housing, and transportation. Two million families have *no income* and totally depend on food stamps. Children and families still cannot afford health coverage and suffer or die from lack of preventive care or treatment for illness or injury. Through hard-won gains in enactment of the Children's Health Insurance Program (CHIP), Medicaid, and the Affordable Care Act (ACA), 95 percent of children are covered; but all three programs are now threatened with destruction, which would harm the youngest, poorest, and sickest children the most.

Still, as in the days of Thurman's childhood and in the days of my childhood, countless children in these most difficult, unjust, undeserved circumstances are bolstered and strengthened, nurtured and protected by parents and others who struggle to counter the world's message and remind their children that they are sacred gifts from God and precious in God's sight.

Even as we bolster children's strength despite those who are doing them wrong, parents and other adults along with young people themselves still must work to *end* the systemic wrongs, cultural disrespect, and racism that permeate our nation. Together, we must work to change the injustice, undo the racism, eliminate poverty, and bring real justice to our nation. As Thurman observed of those with their backs against the wall, "This is the position of the disinherited in every age. What must be the attitude toward the rulers, the controllers of political, social and economic life? . . . In the main, there were two alternatives faced by the Jewish minority of which Jesus was a part. Simply stated, these were to resist or not to resist."[6] For children and families in our day with their backs against the wall, and for all who are serving and advocating and working to not only resist oppression but also to bring forth justice, Thurman's words still resonate and speak with power.

Luther Smith, in *Howard Thurman: The Mystic as Prophet*, reflects on the enduring relevance of Thurman's work and words for those of us working for transformative, prophetic change:

> Although Thurman's followers might question the term, it will prove more useful to speak of him as an American prophet. The adjective "American" is not used, however, to limit the significance of his insights. The prophet's identity is deeply rooted in the history, ideals, hopes, and mission of his culture. Prophets are products of their culture, speaking to specific traditions, problems, and purposes of their culture. Their warnings and urgings deal with particular crises of their particular age.[7]

America is the land of Thurman's nurture and prophetic witness. Thurman proclaims that the mistreatment of the nation's disinherited and acceptance of the will to segregate are betrayals of American and Christian ideals. In the tradition of the Hebrew prophets he calls America and Christianity to recall the sources of their identity: for America the Declaration of Independence and Constitution, for Christianity the inclusive love-ethic.

> Prophetic witness is shaped, made, and enacted in particular contexts, but its influence transcends its space and time. The Hebrew prophets had a prophetic message which informs the commitments of twentieth century people all over the globe. Prophetic witness endures. Time will demonstrate the strength of Thurman's word as a message for all seasons. Prophetic witness has an impact beyond particular contexts, and Thurman's thought should prove relevant wherever humanity is involved with the meaning and formation of community.[8]

It is in this spirit of prophetic witness, and the deep abiding faith of loved ones like my minister father and Thurman's Grandma Nancy, that I seek to bolster leaders around this globe to speak truth to power and stand with those whose "backs are against the wall."

RECALLING CHILDHOOD, REMEMBERING THE CHILDREN: INNER LANDMARKS FOR THE JOURNEY

Howard Thurman's words and wisdom have been part of my life for nearly as long as I can remember. His writings were in my father's study, and I was fortunate to hear him in person when he visited Spelman's chapel. Years later, I was in the Howard Thurman Listening Room in Marsh Chapel at Boston University, where Thurman served as chaplain for many years, and spotted in a glass case the Litany of Thanksgiving that appears at the beginning of this chapter. I copied it down on the spot. My sister Olive later found it in his book *Meditations of the Heart*. Each Thanksgiving when our whole family gathers, often in South Carolina, before our meal we read various inspirational passages and always end with this prayer of thanksgiving. There are many of Thurman's writings that could have served as the focus of my contribution to this volume—*Jesus and the Disinherited*, "The Growing Edge," "I Will Not Give Up," and others. Nonetheless, Thurman's litany of thanksgiving is most fitting for my reflections on "prophetic service and global change" in a volume titled *Anchored in the Current*.

Warmth of Humankind

The ANCHOR of my parents' love, support, and faith is the source of my lifelong commitment to service. In *Lanterns: A Memoir of Mentors*, I wrote,

> I do what I do because my parents did what they did and were who they were. I first saw God's face in the face of my parents and heard God's voice in theirs as they cooed, read, told stories, and sang to me. . . . I first felt God's love in their hands and arms and feet as they held, rocked, bathed, and walked me when I was fretful or sick. I first learned God's caring by watching them care for me and my sister and three brothers and for others within our family and community. . . . I learned to speak the truth because it was expected and enforced in my house. . . . My belief that I and others could do more than complain, wring hands, or give in to despair at the wrongs rife in the world stems from my parents' examples.[9]

In 1984, when I was home for my mother's funeral, an elderly white man asked me what I did for a living. I told him, "I do, perhaps on a larger scale, exactly what my parents did: serve and advocate for children and the poor."

There are countless children who don't experience powerful love and secure anchoring from their parents. Fortunately, some are blessed to find it in grandparents or other relatives, or in a caring teacher, a congregation, or a coach. Every year the Children's Defense Fund honors young people who manage to "Beat the Odds" (even as we are working to *change* the odds) despite having their backs against the wall from poverty, abuse, disability, addicted or incarcerated parents and more. In every instance there has been at least one person—if not a parent then someone else—whose belief in them, care, advocacy, and presence made all the difference. The "warmth of humankind" should be known first in our parents' arms, but if not we have to see to it that every child experiences love from somewhere. Every child needs and deserves that anchor to help them weather the buffeting winds of life.

In another meditation, "The Sacrament of Life," Thurman brings to mind "the little children who are not comfortably housed,"

> who do not have warm clothes to wear, who did not have breakfast this morning because there was no food for them; all of the frightened and lonely and desperate little children, all over the world—we remember them, in our comfort, in our plenty. In the quietness we seek to know how we may learn to be more sensitive, to be more charitable, to be more gracious, to be more sharing, if indeed we are to be true to ourselves. *We make a sacrament of our determination to be better tomorrow than we are today. . . .*[10]

Thurman's litany of thanksgiving includes gratitude for the tears shed and the tears seen. This is no celebration of suffering, but this litany serves as a reminder or affirmation of the profound humanity that unites us and the compassion that connects us. The only way we can keep at this work of prophetic service and pursue transformative change with urgency is to remember what is at stake. There are sacred human beings who hurt as we hurt, parents who yearn for the best for their children as we yearn, and young people who ache to be *seen*—and heard. Whether these young people are in foster care or prison or they look like us or not, they, too, seek to be seen even if their bravado masks vulnerability and pain. For this, we give *thanks* for tears shed. Yes, we give *thanks* for tears we have the eyes to *see*.

In the meditation "Let Us Remember the Children," in *The Inward Journey*, Thurman begins,

> There is a strange power inherent in the spirit of [humankind]. Sitting or standing or lying in one place, he [she] can bring before his [her] presence those who are separated from him [her] by distance or by death, those whose plight he [she] understands but whose faces he [she] has never seen and whose names register in him [her] no meaning. Let us bring before our spirits the children of the world![11]

After calling to mind children in refugee camps, war zones, orphaned or impoverished, those who are unloved or sick, those who are injured or have disabilities, and those who have never known hardship, Thurman concludes with this prayer:

> What we bring before our presence, our Father, we share with Thee in our time of quiet and prayer. We thank Thee for the gift to do this, the strange power inherent in our spirits. Grant that what we see in this way may not leave us untouched but may inspire us to be active, responsive instruments in Thy hands to heal Thy children, to bless Thy children, to redeem Thy children. Amen.[12]

At Children's Defense Fund we have worked hard to help people understand and feel the plight of America's children who may be unseen by many. In our work, we seek to provide greater visibility and voice to America's children by sharing their stories, including them as leaders and participants in gatherings and data-based reports. We have helped community groups plan what we call "Child Watches" that take leaders to hear from children and families who are struggling and those who are thriving. On these Child Watch pilgrimages we talk with these families and those who serve them about what is needed to stimulate positive and lasting change. More recently, through "Family Suppers," we help community members come together to listen and receive guidance from "experts by experience." In these encounters, community members learn what kinds of changes are needed from those who are impacted most directly. Children's Defense Fund's efforts seek to forge relationships, increase "proximity," and strengthen the human capacity to be "active, responsive instruments in [God's] hands" for the sake of God's beloved children.

Lanterns that Illumine Darkness:
Messages of Hope

Like beads on a rosary, Thurman "finger[s] one by one the messages of hope that awaited me at the crossroad," recalling the approval, reassurance, inner moral compass, and spoken or written words that helped him at defining moments. The prayer that came to my lips and to the preface to *Lanterns*, was this:

> O God, I thank you for the lanterns in my life
> who illumined dark and uncertain paths
> calmed and stilled debilitating doubts and fears
> with encouraging words, wise lessons,
> gentle touches, firm nudges and faithful actions
> along my journey of life and back to You.[13]

Anyone on life's journey will encounter crossroads and uncertain paths—but perhaps none more than those seeking to engage in prophetic service and transformative social change. We read about it in the Hebrew prophets' anguished grappling with their calls, despair at intractable societies, doubts that their words would be received. Whether to heed God's call or run headlong in the opposite direction wasn't just a problem for Jonah but also one that all prophetic servants face in their own times, places, and ways.

We like to think that prophets and heroes sail confidently through their journeys; but it is not so. When Dr. Martin Luther King Jr. was beleaguered and attacked for speaking out against Vietnam, as a young civil rights lawyer I sought to offer him some solace by sending him Theodore Roosevelt's statement about credit due to the one who "is actually in the arena. Whose face is marred by dust and sweat and blood. Who strives valiantly, who errs and comes up short again and again. And who, while daring greatly, spends himself [herself] in a worthy cause. . . ."[14]

Another time, I went to visit a deeply discouraged Dr. King on my way home to Mississippi. I was returning from Washington, DC, where I had shared with Robert Kennedy my frustration with how slowly the federal government was moving to get food to hungry children, even after his Senate subcommittee's visit related to child hunger and malnutrition in Mississippi. As I recalled in my book *Lanterns: A Memoir of Mentors*,

Robert Kennedy told me to tell Dr. King to bring the poor to Washington to make their plight visible to the American people and to put pressure on President Lyndon Johnson to respond to their needs. A few hours later I sat talking with Dr. King in his unprepossessing SCLC [Southern Christian Leadership Conference] office on Auburn Avenue in Atlanta. He was depressed and uncertain about where to go next. When I told him what Robert Kennedy had said, Dr. King's eyes lit up and he called me an angel sent by God. Thus the idea of the Poor People's Campaign for which I was honored to serve as messenger was born.[15]

The crossroads we encounter as we seek to be faithful servants are often excruciating because we know how much is at stake, how vital the mission is, that it really matters to get it right not for our own sake but for the children and the cause we seek to serve. Thurman's litany observes that these crossroads moments sometimes call for affirmation from one we respect or encouragement to step forward in the face of our fears. Sometimes we need to be attentive to the voice within or receive a written or spoken word of encouragement. It's paradoxical that "retreat" is often what is needed to be prepared to move forward with urgency and persistence in building the children's movement and pursuing other crucial justice work. A spot in my back garden and a small room off my office have helped me carve out some moments of quiet and prayer needed for discernment at crossroads, as have silent retreats and an annual women's spiritual retreat. Thurman's meditations continue to serve as a lantern of hope for those of us who seek to serve, speak truth to power, and transform our nation and world.

Mainsprings of Our Heritage

In our too-divided nation, we often hear the word "heritage" and assume it's limited to one's own ancestors or one's own "people." Thurman's much more encompassing perspective lays claim to an even wider, richer, more expansive heritage: the generations that came before him, to be sure, but also the seers and prophets, workers and pilgrims, and saviors. As we seek to build a movement and make our nation and world fit for children, knowing our heritage is indispensable. All our children—and we—need to know about the generations that came before: to celebrate, cherish, appreciate what their lives and legacy mean for us, whether it's the brave efforts of the Hebrew midwives

Shiphrah and Puah who defied Pharaoh to save the baby boys; the courageous trips Harriet Tubman made to usher families to freedom along the Underground Railroad; the behind-the-scenes planning that Jo Ann Robinson undertook with Rosa Parks that helped spark the Montgomery bus boycott; the leadership of young people that Ella Baker helped empower from the sit-in movement through the formation of SNCC (the Student Nonviolent Coordinating Committee); or the light of truth and courage that Fannie Lou Hamer shone despite police brutality. Knowing this heritage can embolden and encourage our own efforts.

The profound transformation our nation and world need calls for "seers who see visions and dream dreams"; we cannot acquiesce or resign ourselves to how things are now. Child poverty is not an act of God or an inevitability. It is the result of human choices and unjust political decisions and we can and must choose to end it! Eradication of child poverty won't happen in a day, or a year—perhaps not even in our lifetimes. But it *could* happen if enough of us work with urgency and persistence to achieve it. Transformation calls for servant leaders whose vision, in Thurman's words, "could only find fulfillment in the years which they would never see." If our goal is high enough, dream big enough, hope expansive enough, and courage strong enough, then with persistence and determination it can be achieved. I've kept on my office wall Reinhold Niebuhr's words in *The Irony of American History*:

> Nothing that is worth doing can be achieved in our lifetime; therefore we must be saved by hope. Nothing which is true or beautiful or good makes complete sense in any immediate context of history; therefore we must be saved by faith. Nothing we do, however virtuous, can be accomplished alone; therefore we must be saved by love. No virtuous act is quite as virtuous from the standpoint of our friend or foe as it is from our standpoint. Therefore we must be saved by the final form of love which is forgiveness.[16]

Such love, forgiveness, and vision of transformation remain central to the heritage of child advocacy and care.

Meaning of Our Lives and Commitments

We give thanks for the anchor of family, community, the warmth of humankind, and the heritage of those who came before. And we have our own work to do now. I loved the words of Mrs. Amelia Boynton

Robinson in Selma, who was still sharp of mind and spirit after a century of living. She once said to the many younger generations lauding her, telling her how they stood on her shoulders, "Get off of my shoulders. The foundation has been laid, now it's time for you to build on it. Now, it's your time. Get to work."[17] This leads to the culmination of Thurman's litany: the meaning of one's own life and the commitment to which one gives the loyalty of one's heart and mind. Each of us will answer that differently. What is the meaning of your life and the commitment to which you give your heart and mind?

For me, it has been building a movement for children so that we leave no child behind and ensure every child a Healthy Start, a Head Start, a Fair Start, a Safe Start, and a Moral Start in life and successful passage to adulthood with the help of caring families and communities. The Children's Defense Fund provides a strong, effective, and independent voice for all the children of America who cannot vote, lobby, or speak for themselves; but we pay particular attention to the needs of poor children, children of color, and those with disabilities. Our goal is to educate the nation about the needs of children and encourage preventive investments before they get sick, drop out of school, get into trouble, or suffer family breakdown.

It is unconscionable that our rich nation lets one in five children live in poverty. It is intolerable that our nation, with its advanced medical technology, allows millions of children to lack health coverage and the opportunity to see a doctor for preventive care or receive treatment when sick. It is unacceptable that millions of children are waiting for a quality Head Start or child care program to get ready for school. It is profoundly immoral that we let the lottery of geography or race determine a child's chances in life, as if God created separate classes of children.

When you know the meaning of your life, your purpose, and commitments, there is, as Thurman voiced, "a restlessness which bottoms all I do with its stark insistence that I have never done my best, I have never dared to reach for the highest."[18] Far from bemoaning that feeling of restlessness, Thurman gave thanks for it. I've certainly experienced that restlessness and witnessed it in colleagues, activists, and servant leaders across our country. One doesn't "clock in and clock out" on a calling when there is so much to do, when human lives are at stake, when justice hangs in the balance. Still, it's hard—but important—to take care of ourselves in the midst of impassioned pursuit of justice. Prayer, meditation, and reflections like those from Howard Thurman's heart and hand offer a "centering moment," a reminder of grace, a breath of renewal, and a recognition that we can only do our most faithful best and then turn it over to God. We cannot sustain this work if we are not centered.

I've long had a sense of myself as a seed sower and spreader, recalling the parable (found in Matthew 13, Mark 4, and Luke 8) that recognizes that not every seed sown will sprout, but we must do the work in faith that some will take root. Thurman's resonant meditation "Results Not Crucial" in *The Inward Journey* reminds (with masculine language modified):

> There are many forces over which the individual can exercise no control whatsoever. A [woman] plants a seed in the ground and the seed sprouts and grows. The weather, the winds, the elements, cannot be controlled by the farmer. The result is never a sure thing. So what does the farmer do? [She] plants. Always [she] plants. Again and again [she] works at it—the ultimate confidence and assurance that even though [her] seed does not grow to fruition, seeds do grow and they do come to fruition.
>
> The task of [women] who work for the Kingdom of God is to *Work* for the Kingdom of God. The result of this demand is not in their hands. [She] who keeps [her] eyes on the results cannot give [herself] wholeheartedly to [her] task, however simple or complex that task may be.[19]

The Children's Defense Fund's logo is a child's drawing of a little boat on a tumultuous sea with a fisherman's prayer: "O God, be good to me, the sea is so wide and my boat is so small." Like Thurman, "the big hope that never quite deserts me" is an end to violence and that *our* love and nurture and protection and justice and the grace of God will "cover the life of the children of God as the waters cover the sea." We can't dream small, aim low, or hold back if we are to create the prophetic, transformative change our world needs. Embrace the big hope. What is your big hope?

GROUNDING QUESTIONS

1. Where have you experienced "the warmth of humankind"? How has that warmth influenced your calling to prophetic service and global change?

2. What messages of hope have you encountered at crossroads in your life? How have they contributed to your pursuit of prophetic service and work for change?

3. Reflect on the meaning of your own life and the commitment to which you give the loyalty of your heart and mind. What are the purposes to which you have devoted your love, desires, and gifts? (That's a big question, so really take your time and "linger over" it, as did Thurman.)

4. Where do you experience a sense of never having done your best or dared to reach for the highest? What has constrained you? What could free you to dare to reach?

5. "Prophetic service and global change" inherently call for big vision, hard and daring work, and persistent hope against all odds and often in the face of discouraging present realities. What is "the big hope that never quite deserts [you]" and fuels your prophetic service and work for global change?

6

✢

Where Freedom Forms

Place, Purpose, and "the Particulars"

✢

STARSKY D. WILSON

"A MAZE OF PARTICULARS"

. . . the individual is interested in relieving human need because he [she] sees it as in some definite sense crowding out of the life of others the possibility of developing those qualities of interior graces that will bring him [her] into immediate candidacy for the vision of God. It is in this latter sense that we come upon the mandatory raison d'etre of the affirmation mystic's interest in social change and social action.

He [She] is not interested in social action because of any particular political or economic theory; he [she] is not interested in social action primarily from the point of view of humanitarianism or humanism – as important as these emphases are, but he [she] is interested in social action because society as he [she] knows it to be ensnares the human spirit in a maze of particulars so that the One cannot be sensed nor the good realized.

—Howard Thurman, "Mysticism and Social Change"[1]

Her face was out of place.

On a Monday after work in late July, I decided to stop by the Schnuck's grocery store near the Deaconess Foundation offices to pick up a few items to keep me out of the fast-food restaurants and committed to the better diet my wife wished for me. As I walked across the parking lot from my car, I heard a familiar call, which had become less frequent in recent months.

"Pastor?!" A thin woman standing to the left of the automatic doors queried before I could make it to the sidewalk. "Is that you? You not over there at the church no more?"

By the time I got to the door, I recognized "Tiara" from the times we spent together during my pastorate at Saint John's Church (The Beloved Community). She was one of the neighbors—my congregation outside the congregation—whom I had spent time in conversation and counseling with many times over my ten-year sojourn there. Now, eight months removed from service in that place, I probably hadn't seen her for more than a year.

At first glance, it seemed she may have still been wrestling with the particular threats we worked together to ward off in her life: being unhoused and economic distress that fueled sex work and self-medication with alcohol and drugs. A closer look during the course of our conversation gave further evidence. Her skin scorched from days, like this, outside all day in the burning sun. Disheveled hair and clothing from swift preparation for the day without the benefit of a looking glass. More missing teeth than our last conversation reflected her extended lack of access to oral care and the impact of protracted drug use.

What I figured from my gaze, conversation confirmed. Tiara shared that in a few days (that Thursday in fact) she would undergo surgery to amputate her left leg. While sleeping outside, she was bitten by a venomous brown recluse spider. Without knowing what was fully going on in her body, and as one of the twenty-seven million people in the United States without health care coverage,[2] she went two months with a growing gaping wound in her leg. When the pain, the excretions, and the opening in her flesh became too much to bear, she went to the emergency room. There, just a few weeks before our chance meeting, she received the diagnosis and treatment plan.

"Pray for me, Pastor. It took me a while to decide. But I said I had to go on and do it and leave it to God. The doctor said, she knew it was a lot to think about. But, I'm gonna go on 'cause this leg right here is just dead."

So, in the parking lot of Schnuck's grocery store on that Monday afternoon, I prayed. This prayer began mid-conversation in my mind. Then, we paused and I prayed aloud with her as those around us unloaded grocery carts in their trunks. In a final word about all she was juggling, she told me, "I might need some bus fare when you come out." After our talk with one another and God, I headed into the store.

As I pushed my cart through the aisles, the particulars of Tiara's situation overwhelmed me. I remembered how tough it was for her returning to the neighborhood and family (from detention or attempted escape, couch surfing in other communities) in various cycles during my time at the church. I recalled her earnest desire for dignity and better living conditions. At the time, I couldn't imagine life getting worse for Tiara. But, of course, with the pending surgery, it did.

Tiara and I went our separate ways that Monday afternoon, but every day that week I continued to pray until it hit me really hard on Thursday. Yet, I found solace in the fact that she trusted and wanted to connect with God, as seen in her decision making and her request for intercession. I wondered how much her appeal for me to pray had to do with an understanding of my office and role in her life as pastor. Or was there some calculation that she lacked access to the Divine, or some evasive capacity necessary to settle her heart and steady the hand of the doctor to assure the surgery would go well? Either way, there was something wrapped up in the request and the challenge of her life circumstances that called me again to pastoral duty at the foot of that blood red Schnuck's sign.

ANCESTRAL GLOW: EDEN LECTURES ON PIETY AND PROGRESS

Just six years after Eden Theological Seminary admitted its first Black student, Howard Washington Thurman visited St. Louis to lecture during the seminary's spring convocation. Over the course of four days in mid-February of 1939, he delivered a series of four lectures that have been regarded as "Thurman at his most scholarly."[3] Under the series header "Mysticism and Social Change," he developed an interpretation of mystic practice, considered its symbolism, and examined its relationship to ethics. In the culminating lecture, Thurman speaks of those whom Rufus Jones termed "affirmative mystics," defined as "those who are concerned with working out in a social frame of reference the realism of their mystic experience."[4] Therein, he explores reasons for mystics' action to bring down manifestations of evil and systems of oppression that create difficulties in the lives of individuals and communities.

Taken together, the mystic theologian framed a spirituality which may have been as equally valuable for the German abolitionist ancestors of those gathered in the chapel at that time as it was for those of us shaped by the school's social justice commitments years later to lead churches in communities established by those ancestors.

As an Eden Seminary alum, I bask in the ancestral glow of Thurman's message and the German abolitionists who had earlier gathered in that chapel. Upon graduation, I accepted the call as pastor of Saint John's Church. Our congregation was founded in 1852, one year before Eden Seminary's opening. The church boasted a leader who served a long pastorate, then led the seminary as its president. Fairground Park, the neighborhood around the church, was initially populated by German immigrants and later abandoned by their descendants in familiar patterns of white flight. Now the area, more than 90-percent African American and largely impoverished, is the closest thing Tiara has to a home. Evidently, I am still her pastor, though I no longer formally serve Saint John's Church.

I also happen to be a pastor whose preparation included a unique classroom experience at Eden. In the spring semester of 2007, Dr. Enoch Oglesby, an African American professor of Christian ethics for three decades at the seminary, taught his first and only class solely composed of African American students. It was also the only course I've ever had, in my combined eight years of theological education, where all my classmates were Black. There were eight of us. Over that term we delved deeply into the spirituality and theology of Howard Thurman. Ironically, we never discussed the February 1939 lectures, which had been delivered just feet away from our classroom and published in the seminary bulletin. We did, however, come to explore Thurman as a mystic and prophet. Accompanying our exploration was the scholarship of Dr. Luther Smith, a former African American faculty member at Eden Seminary.

In that classroom (so small that now it serves as an administrative office), our practices and embedded theologies were stretched by the poetry and biography of our guides: Oglesby, Smith, and Thurman. We came to know Thurman as more than a mentor to civil rights leaders and author of *Jesus and the Disinherited*. Within that unique, close-knit community of Black seminarians, sitting at the feet of an elder, learning of the witness of an ancestor, God prepared for me a space and place of formation. Central to that formation was breaking down the silos of false, Western binary thinking between personal piety and social transformation.

A common theme emerged between Thurman's 1939 gathering with the German evangelical community and Oglesby's 2007 eight-student class: a rejection of the false dichotomy between progressive commitments to social transformation and evangelical calls for personal piety. Indeed, these poles still pull at corners of Protestant mainline denominations. They remain present in the United Church of Christ with which Eden is now affiliated. They persist as well in the historic Black church traditions like the Baptist and Pentecostal fellowships represented in that 2007 seminary class.

Here, of course, I recognize the limitations, yet make sense of the commonalities between notions of piety present in German evangelical heritage, personal conservatism in the Black church, and mystical asceticism analyzed by Thurman. Likewise, I recognize nuances in progressive religious movements where macro-level social change becomes an end unto itself. While some evangelicals, like the ones who raised me in church, define mission as the conversion of individuals, progressive Christians, like Martin Luther King Jr., operate largely from a social gospel ethic that sees the redemption of the soul as primary in the work of social transformation.

King, a student of Thurman, engaged in strategies and tactics of nonviolent direct action which sought to win the oppressor's heart as a step in the process of changing systems. In religious thought further to the left, the concept of individual lifestyle change and the engagement in spiritual disciplines in the interest of divine connection is de-emphasized altogether. Herein, it becomes difficult to discern faith-inspired action from progressive secularism simply wrapped in religious language and garb.

To each of us, who come into contact with persons like Tiara who wrestle with social trauma and yearn to connect with something greater, Thurman offers a gift. No matter where we fall on the spectrum of personal piety and social transformation, Thurman's approach through mystical engagement in social action has value and renders loving critique.

> [The affirmation mystic] is not interested in social action because of any particular political or economic theory; [s]he is not interested in social action primarily from the point of view of humanitarianism or humanism—as important as these emphases are, but [s]he is interested in social action because society as [s]he knows it to be ensnares the human spirit in a maze of particulars so that the One cannot be sensed nor the good realized.[5]

Here, Thurman rejects the polarization of spiritual discipline and social action. He also refuses to leverage individual conversion as a simple tool for societal change. Consistent with his mystical commitments, Thurman suggests the ability to achieve and cultivate God-consciousness is primary in the human project. Rather than seeking to change the individual in order to change society, he makes the case that those truly interested in meeting human needs must work to remove the network of oppressive nuisances that inhibit psychic and spiritual ability to see and hear God's Spirit. Liberating people from this "maze of particulars" is the most appropriate alignment of asceticism and action as it leverages social transformation to allow for lives connected to God.

PLACE MATTERS: PLACEMAKING AS RESISTANCE TO THE PARTICULARS

Although he was not traditionally a very devout person, my late grandfather R. L. Turner, with whom I lived for much of my senior year in high school, was a hardworking and wise man. He once told me, "Son, there ain't but three things you've got to do in life. Find your place. Get in your place. And stay in your place." (As you may sense from the tone of these words, he wasn't very happy with me when he dropped these pearls of wisdom.) As a war veteran and son of the segregated South, he realized that understanding place can be a protective factor that preserves life. While I grew up in a different era and under different circumstances, the more I think back over my life, the more I appreciate his words. For me, place has been formative and significant in shaping my call to ministries for justice.

My grandfather's sage words on place have prompted reflections on the intersection of location and vocation. So, I wonder how Thurman thought of his place as mystic and activist? Why did he deliver a set of lectures on activism at Eden Seminary in St. Louis but never publish them for a broad readership? How has place informed my life and work? How much was my vocational trajectory as a minister and activist shaped by the seeds Thurman planted on campus and the conversations that sprouted decades later in that little classroom of Black seminarians? What if I had gone to the store I usually patronize near my house, instead of Schnuck's, that summer afternoon and had never seen Tiara again? Since I only came to know of Saint John's through my studies at Eden, would I have found my way to that congregation (and Tiara) had I not matriculated at this midwestern seminary?

One of the enduring images of Thurman, for me, is that of a young boy in Florida lying in the grass or against the trees gazing up into the skies. It was in those moments, he noted, that he began to sense and explore the unity of all creation in nature. Perhaps it was also there that he initiated cultivation of sensibilities that others will come to identify as mystical. When Thurman was a seven-year-old boy, the pastor of his family church refused to funeralize Thurman's father because his worship patterns were more like those of my grandfather; Thurman found sanctuary underneath the stars at night and with the sounds of the ocean at Florida's coastline. When the church did not offer space for his family, God invited him into new places. It was in those places that he connected with the One.

Place matters. So, it comes as no surprise that Thurman seeded words about mysticism in social change in a St. Louis seminary just 15.8 miles from Canfield Drive? For decades, the roots of activism and mysticism burrowed beneath the Missouri streets. Seventy-five years after the Eden lectures, the word of God spoken through Thurman broke the surface and began to sprout in neighboring town called Ferguson.

It was August 9, 2014, when an eighteen-year-old Black man named Michael Brown Jr. was killed by police officer Darren Wilson. In this historical moment, our community needed the lessons of Thurman's lectures on mysticism and social change. The shooting jolted us. The trauma of seeing Michael Brown lying lifeless in his own blood for more than four hours on Canfield Drive fueled the youth-led Ferguson uprising. This movement captured the imagination of the world, as it called systems to task, challenged clergy to action, and catalyzed a budding movement for Black lives.

Through the Ferguson Commission, which I would be called to lead, the region paused to pay attention to the maze of particulars. On the Ferguson Commission we examined issues ranging from discriminatory criminal justice practices to inequitable educational opportunities. Front of mind for me in each of these conversations was how these unchecked policies make young Black and brown people less likely to realize "the good" to which Thurman alludes. Ferguson sparked local, national, and global debates on race, class, and justice. Yet, it is not lost on me that Thurman tilled the soil for these fearless dialogues seventy-five years earlier. Place matters, and I learned in that classroom on Eden's campus that bourgeoning movement would need carefully prepared places.

Placemaking is an act of God to facilitate connection between humanity and the Divine. These places can be naturally occurring— as evidenced by Howard Thurman's life—or carved out of the natural environment or social order through construction and intention. Curating places beyond the maze of particulars that ensnare the human spirit is an act of resistance, liberating people to experience God.

In his 2018 book *Palaces for the People*, Eric Klinenberg, professor of sociology and director of the Institute for Public Knowledge at New York University, explores how "social infrastructure" helps to heal societal divisions and make communities more resilient. He defines the term as "the physical places and organizations that shape the way people interact" noting that "that when social infrastructure is robust, it fosters contact, mutual support, and collaboration among friends and neighbors."[6] From comparisons of how Chicago neighborhoods fared through a 1995 heat wave to the ways the "small schools" initiatives of the 2000s and reducing campus size increased student graduate rates, likelihood to enroll in college and matriculation at elite universities, the sociologist effectively argues that place and freedom from some of our most intractable challenges are connected.

"Deliberative design" like this can be a valuable input to removing the isolation that leaves someone like Tiara alone to wrestle with life's challenges. It can also create space for community building to facilitate response to flashpoints like police-involved shootings, community violence, or political conflict. These places in community also demonstrate what Walter Brueggemann in *Prophetic Imagination* calls an "alternative witness" to the separation and oppression in wider society.

WHEN HISTORY ARRIVES AT THE CHURCH'S DOORSTEP, OPEN THE DOOR: PURPOSEFUL HOSPITALITY AND SOCIAL CHANGE

An early activation for me during the Ferguson uprising was when Saint John's Church, the place I first met Tiara, opened its doors to the #BlackLivesMatter Freedom Ride to Ferguson in 2014. Our church would also serve as a welcome center for #FergusonOctober in the fall of that year. Over the next four years, we would continue to extend hospitality to movement groups, from the St. Louis Action Council (now Action St. Louis) to Missourians for Alternatives to the Death Penalty. We conceived of our hospitality as a ministry of placemaking.

Even though our ninety-year-old building presented some physical restrictions, opening our church and making strangers into neighbors provided us clarity of purpose.

Kristian Blackmon was a community organizer and a leader in our church. Blackmon, who self-identifies as a Black, queer woman, once remarked that she saw herself in the folks who arrived at our doorstep on the Freedom Ride. The folks who mirrored Blackmon's experience would likely reflect what Thurman called the disinherited. Disinheritance was far from a theoretical abstraction for Thurman, whose boyhood was spent in the Jim Crow South. Blackmon and Thurman would agree that far too many, because of their youth, lack of access to resources, sexual orientation, or gendered identity, are pushed out or marginalized by the church. Saint John's work to make the disinherited like Tiara and activist groups like the Freedom Riders feel welcome garnered appreciation from some and suspicion from others. The ministry of placemaking became critical to our congregation's self-understanding. Further, we extended love and support to visiting activists, for we learned that many would feel the sting of ostracization upon their return home.

Our hospitality in that historic moment would mean a critical escape from particular oppressions for the Freedom Riders. At Saint John's during the Freedom Ride, valuable connections for resilience and resistance were made, as the place had been prepared. I later learned through *When They Call You A Terrorist* that while many young activists knew each other through social media and had communicated by phone, some had never met face-to-face. In fact, on the first night of the Freedom Ride, the cofounders of #BlackLivesMatter Patrisse Khan-Cullors and Opal Tometi met in person for the first time at Saint John's Church.[7] How might the mission and movement of churches around this country be altered if placemaking was fully embraced?

During the Ferguson uprising, God deepened my sense of purpose and deepened my appreciation of placemaking as a ministry of resistance. In creating space for activists visiting Saint John's, I was forced to interrogate my privilege as a straight, male, middle-class clergyperson with access to property and the social capital to insulate me from a network of societal oppressions. Conscious reflection on these privileges clarified my ministry at Saint John's. Such reflection also offered perspective on my work with the Ferguson Commission as I helped to curate social infrastructure and resist the powers that rushed in to harm and hurt our neighbors like Tiara. The meditative practice of reflecting on these particulars kept me from "crowding out . . . the possibility of developing those qualities of interior graces that [would] bring [me] into immediate candidacy for the vision of God."[8] Beyond participating in processes to relieve the tensions of the moment, this had to inform my understanding and reason for social action during the Ferguson uprising.

THE MOUNT OF VISION: FROM THE RED DIRT MOUNDS OF MONTGOMERY TO THE FOOTHILLS OF TENNESSEE

For Thurman, the life of the mystic has promise beyond his or her own peace. For affirmation mystics this promise is manifest in social change which impacts the lives of others. In the language of my southern home church, this promise would be Tiara's salvation from the maze of particulars that ensnares her spirit and restrains her flourishing. But Thurman doesn't end there. The mystic's activity may also be intended to deliver her to "ascend the mount of vision with freedom and abandonment."[9] Thurman's "mount of vision" points to a place of aspiration, an elevated space of hope where God's future and purpose are revealed.

The phrase transports me to a mound of red dirt, littered with bulldozers and protruding concrete relics from buildings that had been razed. I scaled the hill which covered a city block in Montgomery, Alabama, in December of 2015 with a group of faith leaders led on tour by Bryan Stevenson. The attorney and founder of the Equal Justice Initiative took us there to detail a project he was working on to honor the more than four thousand people lynched in America. He also showed us a loading dock on the backside of his office space. This, he said, would later house a museum that would tell the story of the American mutation (or evolution) from slavery to mass incarceration. Both spaces were blank canvasses. But in each he saw with his heart something that did not yet appear to our eyes.

In May of 2018, I returned to Alabama on a pilgrimage with the Children's Defense Fund (CDF) and Jack and Jill of America to honor the fifty-fifth anniversary of the Birmingham Children's Crusade. Before leaving, my family and I drove from Birmingham to Montgomery. First, we visited that old loading dock which at one time processed enslaved Africans. Then we learned together of the social atrocities of lynching in the Legacy Museum, which opened just weeks before. I was moved that at its conclusion is a video and statue titled "For Mike," dedicated to Michael Brown Jr. Then we traveled over to where that mound of dirt was transformed into The National Memorial for Peace and Justice. In this sacred space, my sons read the columns engraved with the names of the lost by hangings: their names suspended in the air and, at times, swayed over their heads.

While difficult for some to experience, for Stevenson the two-part project is an effort to help people see clearly the impact of historical oppression and movement of God in a call for healing. Place matters. In this way, Bryan Stevenson is a prophetic placemaker who carved out a "mount of vision" for all of us. At the memorial, we find a place of solemnity and reflection. In that place, I hear God speaking directly and through the ancestors memorialized there. Of course, memorials are not the only such expressions.

In the hills of Tennessee, Marian Wright Edelman has crafted a mount of vision at CDF's Alex Haley Farm. There faith leaders, a council of elders, college students, and community organizers from across the country make an annual retreat from their daily responsibilities. For nearly a week, this intergenerational gathering of leaders climbs the mount of vision to worship, strategize, and build community while surrounded by nature. In this place uniquely crafted to spark resistance, these leaders reflect on the pressures of powerful social forces and the harsh particulars of everyday life for the disinherited.

The Highlander Research and Education Center is located not an hour away from the Alex Haley Farm. Co-led by Ash-Lee Woodard Henderson and Allyn Steele, the center advances the legacy of the Highlander Folk School, where civil rights leaders like Rosa Parks, Stokely Carmichael, and John Lewis learned and strategized. Henderson once called this place "the Southern movement infrastructure." Far too few know of Highlander's impact on American history. Yet, that place was firebombed by the Ku Klux Klan in 1966 and targeted by arsonists in April of 2019. The Highlander Research and Education Center stands as a reminder that there are political forces and powers of evil that militate against ascent to such mountains.

Thurman's "mount of vision" is more than physical places like the Legacy Museum, Alex Haley Farm, or The Highlander Research and Education Center. The "mount of vision" requires continued efforts to dream and build new futures. In our work for child welfare through philanthropy in St. Louis at Deaconess Foundation, the Ferguson uprising enlightened us about the movement's need for infrastructure. We also came to realize that if people never experienced child well-being and didn't know the language, it could never be. Informed by Haley and Highlander, in 2016 we began building the Deaconess Center for Child Well-Being as a place where connections might overcome isolation and discussion could create an escape from the particulars. Prayerfully, there, the vision of children flourishing will blossom.

Years ago, in that little seminary classroom, Dr. Oglesby explained the kin-dom of God as the "already, but not yet." Many of Jesus' followers experienced this kin-dom as they witnessed healings, encountered miracles, and heard his teachings. The same may be true of the "mount of vision" where physical places touched by ancestors like Thurman and the living God offer the disinherited like Tiara and the Freedom Riders glimpses of God's vision, if only for a few moments.

Thurman's lectures on mysticism and social change. Oglesby's class on Thurman's spirituality and theology. St. Louis's wrestling with the Ferguson Uprising. #BlackLivesMatter's Freedom Ride to Ferguson. America facing the legacy of slavery and incarceration. Civil rights leaders training to change the world. Child advocates connecting to promote the well-being of our young. My ministry to Tiara. Tiara's talk with God. Each of these encounters needed a place.

Place matters. The mount of vision is the place where freedom is formed as people escape the particulars and connect with the power of the One.

GROUNDING QUESTIONS

1. Who in your life comes to mind and heart as you reflect on the particulars of oppressions Tiara must face?
2. What might be "the particulars" crowding out your capacity to welcome neighbors and experience the common good?
3. Where are the places that deepen your sense of vocation and call? Who stewarded or crafted those places and spaces?
4. What purposes does your spiritual life serve for others? What social changes may come forth from your reflective engagement?
5. Why do you engage in social action? How is this connected to your understanding of God and God's activity in the world?

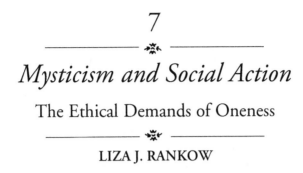

7

Mysticism and Social Action

The Ethical Demands of Oneness

LIZA J. RANKOW

> We must proclaim the truth that all life is one and that we are all of us
> tied together. Therefore it is mandatory that we work for a society in
> which the least person can find refuge and refreshment. . . . [We] must
> lay [our] lives on the altar of social change so that wherever [we] are the
> Kingdom of God is at hand.
> —Howard Thurman, "Religion in a Time of Crisis"[1]

Howard Thurman was born and raised among the working poor in racially divided Daytona Beach, Florida, little more than a generation removed from slavery. In the foreword to his 1965 book *The Luminous Darkness,* Thurman describes the scars that segregation left deep in his spirit and his enduring "sensitivity to the churning abyss separating white from black." He goes on to say, "Nevertheless, a strange necessity has been laid upon me to devote my life to the central concern that transcends the walls that divide and would achieve in literal fact that which is experienced as literal truth: human life is one and all [people] are members of one another." With these words he introduces his reflection on "the anatomy of segregation and the ground of hope."[2] He wrote it as an offering during the height of the southern freedom movement (more commonly known as the civil rights movement) in just two sittings, so indelibly was its message etched within him.

SEEKING WHOLENESS IN A FRACTURED WORLD

From the arrival of the first European ships on the shores of what is now the United States, race has been used as a wedge and a justification for oppression and genocide. Yet Thurman, and many wise souls before and since, have recognized an inherent oneness that breathes through all life and being. Despite growing up under the brutalities of U.S. apartheid, Thurman knew in his bones and in his spirit our profound inseparability from one another. He often noted that "the contradictions of life are not only final but ultimate"[3] and he, as do we, inhabited the contradiction of our fundamental oneness in a world fractured by so many forms of separation and division.

To Thurman, the way to undermine this fracture and work toward restoring (an original and yet mostly unrealized) wholeness was through the cultivation of authentic relationships. His central pursuit was the search for community—the "common ground" (to use his term) among people at the root of our humanness and our spiritual nature. This quest was at the heart of the Fellowship Church experiment in the 1940s. At a time of local, national, and global conflict, the Church for the Fellowship of All Peoples sought to discover whether repeated and consistent experiences of genuine fellowship among people could be more compelling than all that divides them, transcending the barriers of race, religion, nationality, culture, and social class.[4]

Fellowship Church provided a powerful and pioneering witness. But how are we called to live into the "strange necessity" of Thurman's concern in our own times? Twenty-first-century times when state violence and mass incarceration claim the lives of Black and brown people with impunity. When indigenous sovereignty and environmental sanctity are threatened by the hyper-materialism of a capitalist corporatocracy, and economic inequality is at historic extremes. Times when immigrants are vilified and dehumanized, deported or banned. When fear and nationalism are manipulated to justify an inflated military budget and divestment from programs of social uplift. And in these times, too, of growing social movements, united action, and glimpses of hope. It is often out of extremity that possibilities emerge. When the conditions of inequity become dire, more and more people are rattled from their complacency and awaken to the imperative for social change and the restoration of our collective humanity.

Vincent Harding, the great historian and activist, who regarded Dr. Thurman as his surrogate father, tells us that Thurman was profoundly concerned with the social justice activism of his day. In an interview, Harding notes that

> Thurman was a resource . . . reminding us of the wholeness of life.
> He was *with* the Movement, but in a very different way than Martin

[King] was with the Movement, or that Fannie Lou Hamer was with the Movement, or that Ella Baker was with the Movement. He was with the Movement as a manifestation of this *wholeness* that he believed in so deeply. He recognized that what the Movement was doing was not simply trying to get laws passed, but trying to bring a new wholeness to American society. And anything that is working for wholeness, from his perspective, is working for the Divine.[5]

A WORLDVIEW OF ONENESS: MYSTICISM
AND THE MANDATE FOR JUSTICE

Howard Thurman was a mystic. He offered this "working definition" of mysticism as "the response of the individual to a personal encounter with God within his own soul." He adds, "such a response is total, affecting the inner quality of the life and its outward expression and manifestation."[6] Although most often thought of as an intensely private experience, Thurman notes that "even in the moment of vision there is a sense of community—a unity not only with God but a unity with all life. . . ."[7] In my conversations with his daughter, Olive Thurman Wong, she lamented that so many people failed to grasp the centrality of oneness to her father's life and thought. She insisted, "You can't really understand my father unless you understand that point." Of course, "oneness" is an easy enough thing to bandy about. It is even an easy thing to profess, until we realize that it must include not only the people we like and agree with, not only those to whom we are sympathetic, but also those whom we view as abhorrent (whatever side of a political position we may hold). We don't get to choose who we are one with—it's everybody.

But be clear that oneness does not mean sameness. And unity is not uniformity. It is not a homogenization thing. Thurman cherished the unique expressions of every individual and the sacred dance between the particular and the universal. We can regard it this way: the infinite diversity of expression emerges from an infinitely inclusive whole. A divine whole. In a theistic framing, that wholeness is God. And through our oneness with God, everything and everyone—every expression of Life—is one with every other expression of Life. Buddhist master Thich Nhat Hanh uses the term "interbeing" to describe this. Even in science, quantum physicists and quantum biologists point toward a common energetic matrix, and a unifying intelligence within all that is.

This unitive worldview—this worldview of oneness—has profound ethical implications. If all life is one, then there is no "them" separate from some constructed and exclusive "us." If all life is one, we cannot abuse or drop bombs on some "other" people—there is no *other*! We cannot exploit or commodify the earth if the earth is the body of the Divine, part of the oneness. There is no race or class or nation, no river or blade of grass, that is not part of this sacred all-embracing wholeness and ultimately, therefore, part of (whatever I may understand to be) myself. Within this paradigm any act of violence, hostility, oppression, or exploitation is perpetrated against God, against the Divine, against the whole. And any genuine act of loving kindness or service is likewise of benefit to the whole. In a cosmology of oneness, nothing is inconsequential; everything—from the microscopic to the macrocosmic—touches and impacts all things.

In my classes on mysticism and social change, I describe this view of oneness as "north" on the ethical compass of the mystic ethos. (And one need not have had a personal experience of mystic union to adopt this ethic and worldview.) It is something to guide us, to point ourselves toward, to check ourselves against as we work for justice, healing, and liberation. It is the ideal that compels us, although we may never attain it, expanding the radius of our concern and the depth of our responsibility.

MYSTIC AS PROPHET: CREATIVE ENCOUNTERS AND THE WORK OF SOCIAL TRANSFORMATION

Thurman's was a prophetic mysticism that engaged the world rather than withdrawing from it. His mysticism sought to bring the vision glimpsed in what he sometimes called the "creative encounter" into manifestation in human relationships, social institutions, policies, and the practical "for-instances" of our lives. He writes, "What [the mystic] experiences [during the encounter with the Divine] he [she] is under obligation to achieve in [lived] experience. . . . He [she] cannot escape the responsibility of working out the good in a manifold of inner and outer relations. . . . [The mystic] must embrace the social whole and seek to achieve empirically the good which has possessed him [her] in his [her] moment of profoundest insight. In his [her] effort to do this, he [she] constantly checks his [her] action by his [her] insight. It keeps his [her] insight true and his [her] action valid."[8]

There is a stereotype of mystics seeking to escape the world, concerned only with the ecstasy of their own experience of union with the Divine; yet in that union is a doorway that opens out into everything and everyone. The experience of oneness brings us back into relationship with the allness. The oneness and the allness inter-be (to return to the term from Thich Nhat Hanh). Thus we feel deeply the wounds of a battered world, and the suffering and needs of the people—including, as Thurman puts it in *Jesus and the Disinherited*, those "with their backs against the wall"—the disenfranchised, the marginalized and the oppressed. Inaction is not an option. The mystic worldview creates an ethical mandate, and it offers a new way to enter the work of social transformation—from the position of oneness rather than dualism. It shifts the paradigm. So it is not that I am "helping" some other unfortunate somebodies from my position of privilege or superiority but rather seeking to restore a fundamental wholeness of which we are all a part.[9] Thurman often quoted socialist union leader Eugene Debs: "While there is a lower class, I am in it, while there is a criminal element, I am of it, and while there is a soul in prison, I am not free."[10]

In common usage, a "prophet" has come to mean a fortune teller or clairvoyant, but the religious origins of the term in the Abrahamic traditions (Judaism, Christianity, and Islam) relate back to the prophets of the Hebrew Scriptures—those who, emboldened by their own "creative encounters" with God, spoke truth to power for the welfare and liberation of the people. Simply put, prophets *denounce* injustice and *announce* the vision of a new and possible world. Rabbi Abraham Joshua Heschel (a twentieth-century mystic, activist, and scholar in the Jewish tradition) said that prophets "combine a very deep love, a very powerful dissent, a painful rebuke, with unwavering hope."[11]

Luther Smith, in his book *Howard Thurman: The Mystic as Prophet*, notes,

> Thurman's prophetic mysticism stresses the formation of community through a liberation process that includes inner freedom. Inward liberation is not only a prerequisite for social transformation, it preserves the revolutionary sense of purpose after social transformation. Inward liberation keeps struggle (means) from being confused as the objective (ends).[12]

Smith offers the example that the struggle for voting rights for African Americans was not simply about obtaining access to the ballot, but to then use that tool in reshaping society. Voting was a means, not the ends. Veterans of the southern freedom movement are quick to point out that their goal was not simply to obtain civil rights, but that this was in fact a movement for spiritual liberation and to redeem the soul of this nation.

CLEARING THE WAY TO THE INNER ALTAR: SOCIAL ACTIVISM AS A SPIRITUAL DISCIPLINE

To Thurman "the mystic's concern with the imperative of social action is not merely to improve the condition of society. It is not merely to feed the hungry, not merely to relieve human suffering and human misery." He notes, "If this were all, in and of itself, it would be important surely. But this is not all. The basic consideration has to do with the removal of all that prevents God from coming to [fullness] in the life of the individual. Whatever there is that blocks this, calls for action."[13] Thurman spoke of the spiritual disciplines as those practices by which we remove the barriers to our "inner altar"—our place of communion with God. And through this definition, he included activism *as a spiritual discipline*, acknowledging that conditions of social and economic injustice can block both the oppressed *and the oppressor* from, as he put it, "free and easy access" to that altar. He affirmed the necessity to identify with, and work for the liberation and reconciliation of *all* parties in order to restore the beloved community. "It is much easier," Thurman acknowledges, "within the context of mystical piety to identify with the sufferer, the hungry, the poor, the neglected, than with those whose power, privilege and insensitivity are largely responsible for the social ills."[14] However, *both* are cut off from their inner altars, and both must be addressed.

A poignant contemporary example of this can be found in the spiritual activism of the Water Protectors at Standing Rock Reservation in North Dakota, as they worked to halt the construction of the Dakota Access Pipeline (DAPL). The $3.8 billion project was designed to carry crude oil across 1,172 miles, passing under numerous bodies of water, including the Missouri River—violating sacred sites on treaty-protected lands of the Lakota and Dakota peoples and threatening the

water supply for the tribal nations and millions of people living in surrounding areas. In early 2016, not finding protection through legal
means, the first of several camps was established as a center for cultural preservation and spiritual resistance to the pipeline. By September
many thousands of people had gathered, including members of more
than three hundred tribes from across the Americas, along with indigenous peoples of other continents, and non-Native supporters.

Their protest was conducted in a climate of prayer and nonviolence;
prayers not only for the water and the earth and the sovereignty of the
indigenous peoples whose rights and ancestral land were being violated,
but prayers for the militarized police and security guards who fought
against them with firearms and water cannons and toxic gas, prayers for
the executives of Energy Transfer Partners who developed the project,
and the U.S. government officials who were tasked with its regulation.
Their prayers and sacred ceremonies were for the healing of all parties
in service to the well-being of all—both now and for future generations.

This recognition that creative, transformative, and lasting social
change must encompass everyone and everything is evident in Thurman's witness. He affirms,

> Every living thing . . . belongs to every other living thing, and I can
> never be what I ought to be until the last living manifestation of
> Life is what it ought to be. For better or for worse I am tied into the
> idiom of everything that lives. And if I forget this, I profane God's
> creation. If I remember it, I come to myself in you and you come to
> yourself in me.[15]

This is a rigorous mandate, requiring both the cultivation of the inner
spirit and the commitment to a just and ethical social order. For Thurman the two are inextricably linked. The "inward journey" of personal
transformation and the "outward journey" of social transformation,
like the in-breath and the out-breath, or the systole and diastole of the
heartbeat, cannot ultimately be separated. Spiritual practice is important not only for renewal in order to sustain the work of justice making,
but to deepen the place from which we undertake that work, so that
we may bring to it a greater integrity and inspiration. And activism can
be engaged as an integral part of our personal and collective spiritual
formation. Even as we address the urgent realities of present injustice,
we must simultaneously reach beyond them to imagine and bring forth
a new vision for the world.

SUSTAINING THE SOUL OF ACTIVISM: CULTIVATING
OUR CONNECTION TO THE SACRED

There is a saying that "pain pushes until vision pulls."[16] Many of us are drawn to the work of social action out of the suffering or trauma we experience or witness, or out of rage at inequity or harm. But inhabiting the energy of trauma or rage over time can take a heavy toll. In my own life, I played out the split that so many experience: where we have an "activist self" and a "spiritual self." (For some people it is an activist self *or* a spiritual self, often with a lot of judgment cast from one side toward the other!) After years on that roller coaster—alternating periods of intense activism with crash-and-burn health crises and deeply spirit-centered periods of illness and recovery—I decided to explore what an integrated life could be. Howard Thurman was a crucial part of my answer, offering an example of how to embody the both-and of spirituality and social action in a way that feels not only authentic, but sustainable.

It is encouraging to see "self-care" become a topic of conversation and concern among today's activists. Sustaining ourselves, taking time for healing, reflection, and rejuvenation is essential to being effective in our work, and to being a beneficial presence in our communities and in the larger world. Self-care and community care are not separate! But too often self-care is regarded simply as a way to provide short-term relief from stress or to numb the pain—a glass of wine or a beer after a hard day, getting a manicure or massage, or zoning out in front of the television. And perhaps sometimes these may be what is needed in the moment. But I am talking here about something deeper: about how we stay connected to our spiritual Source, Thurman's inner altar, the place within that inspires us to do the work of our calling, and that which allows us to bring our wisest, truest, best selves to it on an ongoing basis.

Genuine sustainability is not just about employing enough self-care practices to keep-on-keeping-on, continuing to do what we are already doing without keeling over, often working in the same dysfunctional and abusive ways. There is nothing transformational about that—for ourselves individually, for our strategies as activists and leaders, for our organizations, our movements, or the world. The real question is, How do we sustain the *soul*—the spiritual center, the higher vision, the deepest heart—that can motivate and inform our work and every aspect of our lives as we embody our commitments to personal and social transformation? In this way all that we do can emerge from, and be nourished by, a sense of connection to something greater, something larger than we are from which we can draw strength—whether that is one another, our Ancestors or cultural heritage, Nature, a Higher Power, God—the Sacred, however each of us may define it.

In light of this it may be helpful to reconsider self-care as "soul-care," or transformational self-care, to indicate the practices that help us establish, maintain, and grow that inner connection. My organization, OneLife Institute (which draws heavily on the teachings of Dr. Thurman), came up with the term soul-care to highlight this distinction. In our workshops we describe it as "the growth, development, and preservation of inner resources that allow you to meet whatever life throws at you with _____ and _____."[17] What goes in those blanks is unique to each person and may even shift from time to time. For me it's *love* and *wisdom*. Those are the qualities that I most hope (and strive) to embody. We can take those words, those qualities, and set them as sacred intentions, allowing them to be our ANCHORs, our touchstones. Indeed, they are already within us waiting to be given full expression.

So the self-care/soul-care question becomes, What practices and choices allow us to live from that place of connection to the Sacred, to cultivate our spiritual qualities and meet whatever life brings with the best that is within us? The need for renewal and maintaining an open channel to the Divine was a concern that Thurman raised with those activists and others who sought his counsel and ministry. How do we nourish the wellsprings of the inner spirit in order to sustain our work for justice and withstand the assaults of the struggle? Some common disciplines include meditation, prayer, reading inspirational texts, music, art, creative expression, yoga, tai chi, or other contemplative practice. Personally, I find some of my sweetest communion in the little backyard garden behind my apartment or walking in the neighborhood attentive to the feel of the sun, wind, rain, and earth, or the fragrance of flowers. Nature is a potent spiritual healer. Thurman's own mystical awakenings were experienced as a young boy seeking refuge in nature. He wrote of the peace he found in the company of his favorite oak tree, and of feeling like he was part of the dark starry nights, the ocean's thunder, the flowing river and the woods. In his later life in San Francisco he cherished long walks along the Pacific and tending his roses.

Where do *you* find water for your thirsty spirit? And what connects you with your spiritual Source? What if you engaged those practices proactively, as part of the daily fabric of your life, instead of waiting until accumulated trauma or burnout take their toll? Not using spirituality as an escape or anesthesia, but as a source of replenishment, insight, resilience? What if we centered those practices collectively and integrated them into our activist movements? Communal spiritual practice—of singing, prayer, and shared worship—was central to the southern freedom movement. And we see it today, for example, in the struggle for indigenous sovereignty and in the movement for Black lives. By bringing spiritual practice into our activism, and embracing activism *as* a spiritual practice, we are transformed as we transform our world. The process is reciprocal.

And we do not undertake this work alone. We have comrades, community, allies and accomplices all over the planet. There is strength and hope in remembering this, and in reaching beyond the manifest world to the larger Life that surrounds us—the forces of Nature, the wisdom of the Ancestors, the power and presence of the Spirit. These too are part of the oneness. A mystic approach to social action invites us to call on energies beyond our finite selves in order to stand with grace, courage, and fierce love, addressing the indignities of the world with a depth that causes them to crumble. Thurman reminds us that God is against all dualisms, and anything that denies the oneness of Life, ultimately, cannot stand.

AN ETHIC AND AN ACTIVISM
DRIVEN BY LOVE

As we lay our lives upon the altar of social change (referencing the epigraph that began this reflection), the goal is not striving to have a mystical experience, but rather seeking to honor the oneness. To live with as much wisdom, compassion, and integrity as we can, mindful that what we do (and what we *don't* do) affects more than just ourselves. Mystic consciousness is the sense of belonging to something greater—not just as an intellectual belief, but a visceral relationship with the Divine in all life. In this context the brutal territorialism of individual, corporate, or national empire building is unconscionable, and every act of oppression or cruelty, a sacrilege. In a worldview of oneness, primary allegiance is not bound by country or creed or culture, or even individualized self-hood, but is to the larger Life, to the sacred transcendent Unity revealing in glorious diversity as the infinite kin-dom.[18]

The mystic ethos invites an ethic and an activism driven by love, and prompts a prophetic engagement with the world. It calls us to become conscious of the entirety of our thought, belief, and action, to seek the places of inconsistency and consider them in light of the larger questions of the meaning of life and the core of our values. There were three questions that Dr. Thurman regularly posed, encouraging people to this deeper reflection. First a question of identity: "Who are you?" (and then a long pause, followed by, "Who are you . . . *really?*"). Next a question of values and purpose: "What do you *want?*" (or sometimes, "What are you *for?*"). Finally, a discernment of means: "How will you get it?" I come back to these questions again and again and again. They are guideposts for me, a way of making sure I am staying true to my own ethical compass, true to the authentic purpose and calling on my life, and ensuring that I respond faithfully—in alignment with this truth—to the exigencies of the world.

Thurman notes, "The time and place of a [person's] life is the time and place of [their] body, but the *meaning* of a [person's] life is as eternal and as significant as with all of [their being they] *will* to make it."[19] This meaning is expressed in the enduring commitments that guide our every step—daring to live more fully, love more deeply, risk more boldly in service to whatever has claimed us, and to give all that we are as a consecrated instrument of healing and justice. In a world where "an eye for an eye" not only leaves everybody blind, but turned to ashes, we must claim a new paradigm—a new covenant with one another, and with all lifekind. I believe that this covenant can be found within the mystic ethos of oneness. Truly understood, it calls us to the highest level of ethical integrity. This is no fluffy feel-good short cut to reconciliation, but a scrupulous demand to do the difficult work of healing centuries of abuse and fracture. The task for each of us will depend on the particulars of our own history, social location, capacities and gifts. The task for all of us is the common project of restoring the sacred wholeness that is our collective truth. Thurman's autobiography, *With Head and Heart*, ends with this affirmation:

> My testimony is that life is against all dualism. Life is One. Therefore, a way of life that is worth living must be a way worthy of life itself. Nothing less than that can abide. Always, against all that fragments and shatters and against all things that separate and divide

within and without, life labors to meld together into a single harmony. . . . In all things there is a secret door which leads into the central place, where the Creator of life and the God of the human heart are one and the same. I take my stand for the future and for the generations who follow over the bridges we already have crossed. It is here that the meaning of the hunger of the heart is unified. The Head and the Heart at last inseparable; they are lost in the wonder of the One.[20]

GROUNDING QUESTIONS

1. What might the mystic ethic of oneness look like in your own life? In your commitment to justice and social change? In your spiritual practice? In your work? In how you eat or shop? In how you vote?
2. What would a commitment to oneness mean collectively? In how we greet one another on the street? In our federal budget? In the national policies we endorse or tolerate?
3. What are the spiritual practices that open the way to your own "inner altar" and keep your spirit renewed and connected with Source? How can you incorporate them into your life on a regular basis?

PART 4

Thurman as Spiritual Anchor

Interlude

Echoes of Head and Heart:
An Ancestral Journey Within

MATTHEW WESLEY WILLIAMS

Sometimes inner resistance is a signal of ground that needs tending. Yes, sometimes that resistance is Care voicing her boundary, holding her ground, "To cross here would be a violation of sacred soil. Back up and come again when the field is ready."

But, tonight I get the feeling that my inner resistance is an invitation to come closer. Approach the sacred soil reverently. Look carefully. Curious trepidation. Sense for Presence.

The ground here is tender.

A delicate chemistry ferments in darkness. Light attention, Presence, letting be with nothing to manipulate or fix. I am here to witness mystery underway. This shadowy terrain repels the anxious heart. Trust hosts guests in this curious space. She alone offers safety in Sheol.

Those shadows, this soil, that ground, the hovering Presence is the subterranean Self; me. Here evil and good lose distinction.

> Grief and joy, no longer distinguishable.
> Love curates the Wisdom rarely spoken . . . in the shadows.
> A different kind of darkness.
> Light turned in on itself.
> A dense sense-awakening darkness,
> Dimensions of me.

Energy radiates, illuminating the outer edge of this fertile ground. A warm mist forms and rests in a cloud just above the soft soil. A chorus of voices emerge from the darkness to question in unison, "Who are you? Why have you come here?"

I have heard these echoes in my head, my heart, since I could translate sensation into sound. Each cry, each coo, each word and moan, an attempt to answer the echoed chorus. Though always with me, I could never locate the sound's source. Until now.

Standing here, surrounded by shadowed darkness and grounded on the sacred soil of my subterranean Self, I see and hear. Calling forth from Sheol the ancestors beckon.

No direction or instruction. They guide through inquiry. They trust my hunger. From the shadows they call, "Who am I? Why have I come here?"

Medicine condenses from the mist as droplets form on my skin. Their query calls me to discernment. This journey of discernment calls me to deep memory.

8

"The Growing Edge" of Life and Ministry

LUKE A. POWERY

ENCOUNTERING
"THE GROWING EDGE"

All around us worlds are dying and new worlds are
    being born;
All around us life is dying and life is being born.
The fruit ripens on the tree;
The roots are silently at work in the darkness of the
    earth
Against a time when there shall be new leaves, fresh
    blossoms, green fruit.
Such is the growing edge!
It is the extra breath from the exhausted lung,
The one more thing to try when all else has failed,
The upward reach of life when weariness closes in
    upon all endeavor.
This is the basis of hope in moments of despair,
The incentive to carry on when times are out of joint
And men have lost their reason; the source of confidence
When worlds crash and dreams whiten into ash.
The birth of a child—life's most dramatic answer
    to death—
This is the Growing Edge incarnate.
Look well to the growing edge![1]

EXPLORING "THE GROWING EDGE"
OF HOWARD THURMAN'S LIFE AND MINISTRY

Worlds die and worlds are born. People die and people are born, every day. When one day ends, another day begins. Every day brings little resurrections of new life, yet on that same day, death comes; "life is dying." This continuum of life and death was what Howard Thurman experienced in his own life. His autobiography, *With Head and Heart*, captures life-altering experiences that shaped his thought and action.

When Thurman was a seminary student, he served as an assistant to the minister at First Baptist Church of Roanoke, Virginia. At some point, the head minister and his family took a vacation, and Thurman was entrusted as the sole minister in charge. During his first night as minister in charge, Thurman was awakened by a phone call from a local "Negro" hospital. A patient was dying and asking for a minister. Thurman rushed to the hospital and once he entered the room, the dying man "in a barely audible voice" questioned, "Do you have something to say to a man who is dying? If you have, please say it, and say it in a hurry." After responding with an "Amen" to Thurman's prayer, the transitioning soul offered the following words, "Thank you. I understand." Thurman recounts, "He died with his hand in mine."[2] In his second decade of life, through this bedside encounter, Thurman was touched by death, literally.

This ministerial moment brought to mind the death of his father seventeen years earlier when Thurman was seven years old. Thurman recounts hearing "the death rattle in his [father's] throat" as he died of pneumonia.[3] He heard death, literally.

Throughout his life Thurman developed a sensory relationship with death. During his childhood in Daytona Beach, Florida, the fatal kiss of typhoid fever gripped his community. "Death was no stranger to us. It was a part of the rhythm of our days."[4] It was a part of the rhythm of his life. This same rhythm pulsed throughout his days. A beloved stepfather, Mr. Evans, died. A respected mentor, Dr. Cross, died.

While death was prevalent, there was far more than loss in Thurman's life. When he was a teenager on his way to Florida Baptist Academy in Jacksonville, he got into a bind at a train station by not having money to send his packed trunk to his final destination. A stranger saw him crying and eventually paid to send his trunk to the destination. To Thurman, this man "restored [his] broken dream."[5] Life was born for Thurman in that moment and he had "the incentive to carry on."

At other times on Thurman's journey life and death stood side by side. When his first daughter, Olive Katherine, was born, his wife, Katie Kelley, fell ill. In order to receive treatment, Kelley returned south with the newborn and left Thurman to continue his work. Katie Kelley eventually lost her health battle and died, leaving Thurman to care for the baby girl. At Olive's birth, because of his wife's circumstances, he notes, "Our joy was short-lived."[6]

After his wife's passing, Thurman took some time to travel and get his bearings. On these travels he learned "that I need never fear the darkness, nor delude myself that the contradictions of life are final."[7] With "the extra breath" to keep living, he married Sue Bailey. Thurman understood from his existential realities that "All around us worlds are dying and new worlds are being born; / All around us life is dying and life is being born." This poem, "The Growing Edge," was about his life, but also the human life we all share.

Thurman also found life in his companionship with nature. He communed with the night, the ocean, the oak tree, and even the rolling storm. He was embraced by nature, causing him not to be overwhelmed by death in the grand scheme of life. Through these deep roots in nature he came to know death and storms as inevitable realities. From this vantage point, he learned not to fear death because ultimately "the growing edge" emerges from obscurity and becomes incarnate.

Not only did Thurman's life reveal the growing edge, but he frames his ministry, particularly corporate worship, under the same umbrella. This poem, "The Growing Edge," appears as an epigraph to a sermon collection by Thurman with the same title, *The Growing Edge*. This poem and book title function as a lens through which to read the entire sermon collection, which is his only printed sermon collection. As Thurman notes in his preface, written while he was Dean of Marsh Chapel at Boston University in 1956, the sermons were preached in the context of worship experiences from a variety of congregational settings—college, university, prep school chapels, Jewish synagogues, Protestant churches. Regardless of the setting, he viewed the sermon as an act of worship and because of the overarching title of the book and epigraphic poem, sermons in the context of worship and the overall worship setting are a milieu for the growing edge to manifest.

Moreover, if there is any doubt of the meaning of the book's title or the poem itself, Thurman includes a last sermon in his book titled "The Growing Edge." I see Thurman beginning the book with the epigraphic poem and ending it with a sermon of the same title as intentional. Growth is the beginning, the ending, and everything in between. His last sermon provides a homiletical interpretation of the poem and asserts more plainly what is the meaning of the growing edge.

His final sermon in the collection, "The Growing Edge," brings clarity about the phrase, if any was needed. Thurman preaches, "No expression of life exhausts life"[8] because there is a brooding life-giving presence that no experience can exhaust. We are not prisoners to any event. For Thurman, the growing edge shows up all throughout life and to him, the resurrection of Jesus is a sign of this. Thurman brings his message of Jesus' hope home at the end of this sermon by saying, "When I die, I will go down to the grave with a shout, because life is not through even in death. Life has an infinite creative possibility. This is what Jesus discloses in his trumpet call, 'I am the Resurrection and the Life. He who believes in me will never die.'" This is the growing edge. It will never die for life is infinite.

ENCOUNTERING THURMAN'S "GROWING EDGE" IN MY OWN LIFE AND MINISTRY

"The Growing Edge" poem causes me to encounter my own memories of death and life. I, too, grew up in Florida like Thurman but in the city of Miami. I come from a people who know the sea. The ocean and its melodic waves beckoned to me as I grew up as well. Its sound. Its smell. Its power. Its vastness. To this day, I still yearn to be close to the ocean because it draws me home. Home is near the ocean, and its waters draw me to remember the transformation of my own baptism. Through these baptismal waters, I draw closer to the growing edge where life dies and life is born. The ocean reminds me of my beginnings.

The calm and forceful Atlantic also leads me to reflect on the water of my mother's womb, from which I entered life. When I was born, I was fully alive and an impetus to joy. Yet the rough waters of my birth unsettled my mother, and she has had high blood pressure ever since I breathed my first breath. One incident in particular caused her blood pressure to skyrocket. One afternoon, while resting in my mother's arms as an infant, I began to struggle to breathe and I convulsed due to a very high fever. One of my older brothers had just arrived home from school and saw what was happening. He picked up the phone and called my father while crying and said, "Luke is dead. Luke is dead." The ambulance came and rushed my mother and me to the hospital while my father met us there. At some point after our departure to the hospital, a neighbor came upstairs in our duplex to see the cause of the commotion above her. When she arrived upstairs, she discovered that the noise she heard was that of my four siblings—ages fourteen, twelve, eight, and four— pacing the floor, praying for me. As a baby, my life was touched by death and life-giving prayer. When the fever broke, I found new life, literally. Word spread throughout the community of the medical care and the fervent prayers of my siblings. Both were key to my survival, to my life.

I remember the cloud of witnesses that have stood with me at critical moments of life and death when I could not stand for myself. Like the many luminaries who graced Thurman's life at different points, I remember my maternal aunt, who moved in with us to care for my mother when she fell and hurt her back during my elementary years. In my youth, my mother's fall had a greater impact on me than Adam and Eve's "fall," that is, their bad decision, in the garden of Eden. My mother's fall was a microdeath, that robbed her of full mobility. Yet, we drew life-giving hope from a community of faith and love that surrounded her and us and continues to do so.

Other signs of life amid death from my childhood to the present have been formative on my journey. Years ago, when my ten-year-old niece died, my wife was pregnant with our son. Our son now carries in his middle name the male version (Christian) of my niece's first name, Christiana. The birth of my son was a "dramatic answer" to the death of Christiana, just a few months earlier. In these two children, life was dying and life was being born.

The growing edge has not only been present in the personal realm but also in the professional domain. When I arrived to serve as the Dean of Duke University Chapel at Duke University in 2012, I was the first black dean to do so. As the "first" in this role, I drew a lot of attention. Given my experience, I can imagine how Howard Thurman must have felt when he was named the first black dean of Marsh Chapel at Boston University nearly six decades before me. When Ms. Lucy Lincoln, the widow of the famed African American sociologist C. Eric Lincoln, first came to Duke Chapel, she made a joyous connection between my appointment as dean at Duke University and her experience of Howard Thurman at Boston University. Together, we broke barriers. This is the growing edge.

In my coming to Duke, a new world was being born at this major research university in the South. At the same time, other worlds were dying. Living into being the "first" was exhausting initially in light of all of the transition and newness. But, I recall receiving an "extra breath" through the inspirited words of Dr. Maya Angelou when in 2012 she spoke to the first-year Duke students inside Duke Chapel, a space where Thurman preached twice in the late 1970s. Her focus was on "the rainbows in the cloud." Those words pierced my soul to give me "the basis of hope" in a new strange land. It was the encouraging word that reminded me of the fruit that would eventually ripen on the tree over time.

In this Dean of the Chapel role and ministry, which Thurman held first at Howard, and then at Boston University, I encounter people from all walks of life—students, staff, faculty, community members, high church, low church, and no-church folks. In this university setting, Duke Chapel stands at the center of campus, at a crossroad. At this neo-Gothic crossing, I encounter life and death by officiating weddings and presiding over funerals and memorials. Regularly, I experience the great joy of teaching and learning and the trauma that befalls an unexpecting community member unaware. One day could be filled with wonderful excitement over a sports win, while the next day can be shadowed with lament over a campus tragedy or a national calamity. The pastoral life exists at the intersection of life and death; it exists at the crossroads of the growing edge.

At Duke Chapel, my primary responsibility is presiding and preaching at worship services. Here, congregational worship is the source and summit of our work and ministry on campus, in the community, nation, and world. Although the chapel has many ministries among students and in the community beyond Sunday worship, worship tends to be the public face of the chapel. There, you will see the community gather and scatter. There, you will hear words through sermons, Scripture readings, and prayer. There, you will eat a holy meal of Communion. There, you will sing and make music through voice, body, and instruments. There, we present our bodies, our whole selves, as living sacrifices, which means all our humanity is offered, all that is dying and all that is being born. This Dean of the Chapel role also provides opportunities for teaching, writing, and research as a professor, similar to Thurman's experience. All its facets, however, live in the ebb and flow of the growing edge because this university ministry is more about stewarding our mortality than morality.

Beyond the personal and pastoral, the professorial role of teaching and writing has also borne scholarly fruit through the growing edge. In terms of scholarship, the growing edge reveals itself in the study of the spirituals. There are only a few theological works on the spirituals, including Thurman's *Deep River* and my own *Dem Dry Bones*.[9] Both of us write about how life and death are intermingled in the spirituals with hope ultimately triumphing. For the enslaved, life was "out of joint" while there was still "the upward reach of life." This disinherited community is a resource of hope and for thinking about life and death, "the basis of hope in moments of despair." The spirituals, as songs of the spirit created in a community, are musical representations of the growing edge; against all odds, the enslaved could still sing and make music as a nonviolent weapon. They sang in sorrow. They hoped in the midst of a hellish situation. They believed that their circumstances did not circumscribe the liberating work of God, and thus they could sing, "There is a balm in Gilead." There was no question as raised by the prophet Jeremiah—"Is there no balm in Gilead?" (Jer. 8:22). Rather, they implicitly asserted courageously, "Look well to the growing edge!" The spirituals reveal how death cannot exhaust life because "hope is a song in a weary throat."[10] The growing edge rises through a melody in life and in death. It cannot be stopped. It will not be stopped because life sings an eternal inexhaustible hymn.

EMBRACING "THE GROWING EDGE"
OF LIFE AND MINISTRY

This Thurmanesque way of viewing life and ministry through the lens of the growing edge is refreshingly relevant for today. First, Thurman presents *the ministry of congregational worship as a critical site of the growing edge* by framing his sermon collection as such. In an age when worship and worship music are commercialized and commodified, Thurman moves us beyond worship as entertainment to its core character of being a matter of life and death, which everyone is dealing with in their own lives but also in the nation and world. Regardless of the musical style, from the volume of a shout to the genuineness of silence, "roots are silently at work in the darkness of the earth." No matter how diabolical the evil is that pervades society, the roots of a watering Holy Spirit are growing to form new life. The ministry of congregational worship reminds us that at the heart of life, there is the heart of God that always beats with love for us. Beyond music, preaching, prayer, preludes and postludes, worship is the place where life and death meet. There, we encounter Reality and are challenged not to underestimate what happens there as mere routine. Thurman helps us probe deeper into human reality and divine reality and does not get consumed with the cosmetics of the liturgy but embraces a larger vision of worship that leads people to the center, regardless of their tradition or denomination. For anyone and everyone in worship, worlds are dying and worlds are being born, making it a context for transformation, not a concert performance.

Second, *the ministry of congregational worship is the site of honesty and truthfulness about death and life.* The growing edge acknowledges mortality. It is honest, truthful, raw, and transparent. There are no clichés about being "blessed and highly favored" or "when the praises go up, the blessings come down." Rather, it asserts the brutal reality about exhausted lungs, weariness, moments of despair, and worlds crashing. Worship, through this lens, acknowledges fragility and failure. "Dreams whiten into ash." This is liturgical honesty rather than hiding behind cute ecclesial phrases of "Christian-ese." This approach to corporate worship allows communities to honestly express dismay, anger, and lament at ongoing racism and injustice across the nation and world. It allows voices to speak out and up about how "life is dying" in prisons or on the streets or in our homes. This worship stance within the growing edge probably will not sell well in the stores of our contemporary society, but it is the very truth that will set us free.

At the same time, worshipers can be truthful that although "worlds are dying," "new worlds are being born." All is not lost because "life is being born." "Fruit ripens on the tree." All is not loss in death, grief, or despair. Although some things die, other things will live. There will be "new leaves, fresh blossoms, green fruit." The growing edge of worship helps us comprehend how we bring our whole selves into the worship setting, the parts of ourselves or the world that are dying and the aspects that are being born. In fact, the growing edge reveals how rites of worship operate at the intersection of death and life. For instance, baptism is a rite in which one dies in Christ and rises in Christ. It is death and life, together. The Eucharist, or Communion, is not only a table of life; it is also a table of death if we take the apostle Paul's words seriously about the table: We "proclaim the Lord's death until he comes" (1 Cor. 11:26).

This honesty about death and life is not a solitary experience but happens within community. This leads to the third point, that through this growing edge lens, *the ministry of congregational worship is a site where a community gathers to mourn and celebrate.* Framing congregational worship under the umbrella of "the growing edge," as Thurman does, implies that this experience of life and death is a communal phenomenon. Worship affirms that life and death join us together in common humanity. "All around *us* . . ." is how Thurman begins. It is not "all around me," but "us." The growing edge of life and ministry includes the community of humanity. It can be in "the moments of despair" or "the source of confidence," in the ups or downs of life and death. Thurman had a strong sense of the communal identity of worship. In his autobiography, he writes,

> In the fellowship of the church particularly in the experience of worship, there was a feeling shared in primary community. Not only did church membership seem to bear heavily upon one's ultimate destiny beyond death and the grave; more than all the other communal ties, it also undergirded one's sense of personal identity. It was summed up in the familiar phrase "If God is for you, who can prevail against you?"[11]

In sickness and in health, in dying and in living, worship is a communal affair.

This is critical in a "selfie generation." In the selfie technological orbit, it might appear that we live to see ourselves because life is all about the self, the individual. "See *my* new haircut. See *my* new outfit. See *my* bircher muesli breakfast. See *my* dog sleeping. See *my* dog jumping. See *my* dog wagging his tail. See *me* with *my* dog. *I* just woke up. *I* just returned from a jog in record time. *I* just repainted and redesigned my office. See *my* office." It is a "see me" era and the technological gadgets have rightly been called "iGods."[12]

iBook, iMac, iPod, iPhone, iPad. *i,* not *we,* not "all around *us.*" When Steve Jobs first introduced the iMac in 1998, he said that the *i* stood for internet, individual, instruct, inform, inspire. If one bows to these iGods, it may feed into the overemphasis on that little, lowercased *i.* It is little because perhaps we have been reduced to a smaller size following these gods, particularly the individual *i* that is consumed by selfies when we really should be gazing at the face of God, the wholly other, and the other who is created in God's image. This is true for life and ministry—the need to transcend the *I* in order to find *us.* Thurman casts "the growing edge" theme over the entire worshiping community, not just one individual, because we all know life and death and are called to rejoice with those who rejoice and mourn with those who mourn.

In community, therefore, *the ministry of congregational worship is, fourth, a site of persistent hope.* In discussing his congregation in San Francisco, Thurman said,

> Our worship became increasingly a celebration before God of life lived during the week; the daily life and the period of worship were one systolic and diastolic rhythm. Increasing numbers of people who were engaged in the common life of the city of San Francisco found in the church restoration, inspiration, and courage for their work on behalf of social change in the community. The worship experience became a watering hole for this widely diverse and often disparate group of members and visitors from many walks of life.[13]

In the "watering hole" of worship, hope rises that causes people to keep on keeping on even "when worlds crash and dreams whiten into ash." People still sing, pray, preach, encourage one another, and show up on Sunday mornings or Wednesday evenings or Friday nights. Something draws us. Someone draws us, to the place of hope in the world. Through various actions of worship, the growing edge is experienced despite it all, and because of it, people can carry on in their lives with one step in front of the other into God's future. Worship provides the "extra breath" for worshipers to move forward in life come what may. Perhaps this perspective will help people not view corporate worship as a pro forma affair, but one that is key to life and living in the world, integrating the liturgy and the liturgy after the liturgy. The various means of communal worship are important but even more so is the end of hope in the human heart. Thurman reminds us that worship is a midwife of hope so that hope unborn will never die again.

The growing edge is present in life and in ministry. For Thurman, he even found companionship and hope in oak trees throughout his childhood. The growing edge is everywhere if we have eyes to see, even in trees. In March 2000, horrendous floods hit the country of Mozambique, leaving many homes and lives threatened and lost. It was a sea of death, literally. Life was dying. One woman, Ms. Pedro, climbed into a tree for safety and shelter once the floods overwhelmed her home. Some of her relatives, including her grandmother, were killed in the floods. Worlds crashed. Ms. Pedro was in the tree for three days and near the end of her time in the tree, the unimaginable happened—she gave birth to a daughter.[14] An African tree became a contemporary tree of life. Life was also being born. Roots were silently at work beyond human sight. In the midst of the groaning of creation, in the midst of a sea of death, labor pains gave birth to life and love in the form of a newborn baby. Fruit ripened on a tree, literally, through "the birth of a child—life's most dramatic answer to death." This is a poignant example of "the Growing Edge incarnate." Hope wins. Life wins. God wins. "Look well to the growing edge!"

GROUNDING QUESTIONS

1. What memories or experiences of life dying and life being born sustain you and those you love?
2. How does "the growing edge" of worship compare with your experience and/or understanding of congregational worship?
3. What are the fruits of your "growing edge"?

9

In Search of Thurman's Apostles

PATRICK D. CLAYBORN

"Seek and you will find."
—Matthew 7:7 NIV

INTRODUCTION

In July 1944, Rev. Dr. Howard Thurman became the copastor (and some years later the sole pastor) of the Church for the Fellowship of All Peoples. I write this chapter from my pastor's study on a summer afternoon in Baltimore, recognizing that it is the seventy-fifth anniversary of Thurman's first Sunday at the church. Thurman faced trials in San Francisco that mirror challenges facing our country today. For his part, Thurman began this segment of his pastoral ministry by calling for the Apostles of Sensitiveness to rise up and fight the good fight of faith.

Since our country is facing corresponding issues to what Thurman confronted, it behooves us to respond as Thurman did. We, too, must call for apostles to rise up. Yet, this mission invites the questions: Where are they? How do we find them?

The purpose of this article is to identify Thurman's Apostles for our present age, and develop a strategy to locate them.

SIMILAR CONTEXTS

Thurman's ministry with the Church for the Fellowship of All Peoples (Fellowship Church) is cast in the backdrop of World War II.[1] Two contextual dynamics were central to this ministry during the early

145

1940s in San Francisco: the disenfranchisement of Japanese Americans and the influx of African American residents. "San Francisco's black population . . . increased by over 600 percent during the war. . . . The rise of black San Francisco was overlaid on the tragic war-time plight of West Coast Japanese Americans, who had been forced by the War Department to abandon their homes and to enter internment camps."[2] Furthermore, the racial tensions between African Americans and whites were high. On the surface, San Francisco seemed to be a place of opportunity and equality for African Americans; however, countless African American San Franciscans felt the daily sting of discrimination. Many feared that San Francisco was on the verge of a race riot.[3]

Seventy-five years later, the backdrop to Fellowship Church is eerily similar to the crisis the United States faces today. The current presidential administration has made drastic changes to the nation's immigration policies and practices. Scores of immigrants are being detained at the borders for seemingly endless periods of time, separated from family members, and kept in deplorable conditions. Many (including children) are in cages and go days without proper hygiene.[4]

While some may argue that race relations in the United States have made significant progress, racism still functions at a high level. The works of Michelle Alexander's *The New Jim Crow*, Ta-Nehisi Coates's *Between the World and Me*, and Carol Anderson's *White Rage* point to the very notion that twenty-first-century racism has taken on different forms.[5] The rash killings of unarmed African Americans by law enforcement over the last seven years articulates racism's unfaltering presence.[6] As a result the Black Lives Matter movement emerged as a national outcry against violence aimed at black and brown bodies.

A number of other atrocities also plague the United States. For example, far too often, human trafficking goes unchecked; violence and discrimination against LGBQTIA communities remains undocumented; sexist practices in the workforce persist that allow women who do the same jobs as men to get paid less; women's rights over their own bodies are stripped away by antiabortion laws; many women continue to face obstacles to reporting sexual violence. Today, the United States even faces seeming interference with American democracy by foreign powers. These issues are obvious barriers to justice, peace, and unity in this nation.

Again, the contexts seem to mirror each other. Compare the two touch points: (1) Japanese American internment camps in San Francisco during WWII with present-day cages at U.S. borders filled with immigrants suffering from malnourishment and the absence of access to basic hygiene and (2) discrimination against African Americans in Thurman's days with the current discrimination against so many minorities. Since the issues look alike, will the proposed solutions be similar as well?

APOSTLES OF SENSITIVENESS

Thurman preached his first sermon at Fellowship Church on July 23, 1944. It was titled "The Tragic Sense of Life." Here is Thurman's summary of his sermon:

> I used Phil 1:9–11 as text developing the idea of the tragic sense of life—the phrase taken from a page I read from Lewis Mumford's Herman Melville. The tragic sense of life arises from the fact that man's [and woman's] higher dreams are always undergirded by the possibility of the lack of attainment. What we see we are not quite able to achieve. The margin of error never disappears.
>
> Next I develop the necessity for love's making for a conscience of the mind as well as a conscience of the heart. The conscience of the heart finds wisdom for the conscience of the mind. *Apostles of Sensitiveness* must do that—be wisdom for the planners and designers and operators of society.[7]

Thurman's inaugural message looks at the ills of society from the lens of a tragic life—one that is not able to reach one's dream. Thurman's answer to this illness is love creating a conscience of mind and heart—with the heart informing the mind. Thurman sees the Apostles of Sensitiveness as the conscience of the heart—informing the designers of society.

Thurman returns to this idea of Apostles of Sensitiveness in his speech "The Cultural and Spiritual Prospect for a Nation Emerging from Total War."[8] He asserts that these persons are needed to rescue the nation from a destructive culture of war:

> Those individuals who by their ability and skills will be at work in various . . . areas of the national life, doing their jobs but who at the same time are ever on the alert to preserve those ideals and ideas of democracy which are being directly threatened at the points where they themselves have power or can exert . . . influence.[9]

Essentially, Thurman suggests that the Apostles of Sensitiveness hold the country's "feet to the fire" making sure that the country lives up to the ideals espoused in the heart of its founding documents: the Declaration of Independence and the Constitution. Thurman notes that minorities are apt at becoming Apostles of Sensitiveness. Their awareness of the need for freedom is heightened because they are most often oppressed by the corrosion of the country's standards for liberty.

Thurman expands the description of the Apostles in his sermon "Apostles of Sensitiveness."[10] The "Apostles of Sensitiveness must have a highly developed sense of fact with reference to other people."[11] Apostles with a heightened sense of fact about others are highly empathetic. With this heightened sense, they do everything in their power to understand the other from the other's point of view, and they treat the other person as one of high regard.

Additionally, the Apostles "have a keen sense of alternatives."[12] They do not submit to the idea that life is frozen and static; rather, they see the world as full of possibilities. No matter how fixed the situation may seem, the "Apostle of Sensitiveness knows that something can always be done, for he [or she] knows that the sense of alternative is the true incentive to social change. . . ."[13]

Thurman also highlighted that the Apostles of Sensitiveness carry a "sense of the future."[14] They are not bound to limiting traditions, resting on their laurels, or settling for consensus when a stance must be taken. To the contrary, the Apostle realizes that there is more in the days to come: more work, more opportunity, more growth, more insight, more creativity, more ideas, and more chances for something new and different to take place.

Finally, Thurman saw these Apostles of Sensitiveness as the keys to changing society. For him, they carried the mantle of combatting racism and militarism, and subverting the destructive culture of war and growing insensitivity among people. In Thurman's opinion, the Apostles would be so inspired to cultivate positive change, foster hope, and create goodwill that they would not rest until they performed their duty.

Uniquely gifted to empathize, seek alternatives, see beyond the present, and work for change, the Apostles of Sensitiveness, Thurman posited, have the capacity to resolve generational woes and heal untreated wounds. Who are the Apostles of Sensitiveness in the United States? How can they heal generational woes and untreated national wounds? How/Where do we find them?

SEARCHING FOR THURMAN'S
APOSTLES OF SENSITIVENESS

Given this nation's challenges with race, immigration, gender, sexuality, sex trafficking, and political divisiveness, the Apostles of Sensitiveness appear to be a worthy choice to aid the United States in realizing the democracy found in the heart of its founding documents. Apostles of Sensitiveness—persons motivated by love who want to inform the minds of those giving structure to our society, who will hold leadership accountable, who are truly empathetic to others, who believe that the goal can be accomplished, who know that there is always more in the future—these Apostles are fully capable of reshaping our landscape.

To begin our search for the Apostles of Sensitiveness in our day, we must first interrogate the name. Would these leaders be called Apostles of Sensitiveness today? The term may have worked well in the 1940s, but would it be received well in our day? Perhaps a better designation would be "Agents of Compassion and Justice." The change in nomenclature can be helpful on two fronts. The switch from apostle to agent may be helpful to those outside the walls of the church. While the titles are quite similar in definition (proponent, advocate, messenger), the idea of apostle is so intimately linked to church that those not familiar with church language may not gravitate to the title. Agent, on the other hand, seems better suited for those outside and within the church zone. Similarly, the change from sensitiveness to compassion and justice is the result of how loaded the term sensitive has become. In this current time, being sensitive can often have a negative connotation and be conceived as highly and adversely reactionary, easily affected by the slightest gestures, and extremely delicate. While this meaning was not Thurman's intention, some in today's society may focus on the negative before hearing the depth of Thurman's idea. Thus, compassion and justice become a better option, since their meanings are a bit more clear.

Thurman does a masterful job in describing the Apostles; however, he never explicitly suggests how one finds them. Thurman states that it "is our common task to enlist all men [and women] of good will . . . in the ranks of the Apostles of Sensitiveness who with rare courage and scintillating insight will dare to define . . . the American way of life. . . ."[15] He also points toward minorities. Their experiences in the failures of the country toward them makes them most qualified to direct how change should take place.[16] With this in mind, how do we find Agents of Compassion and Justice in this day and time?

Following Thurman's lead, one can find Agents of Compassion and Justice by enlisting minorities. Some movements are already present: Black Lives Matter, Gay Pride, teams going to the borders to aid suffering immigrants, and movements fighting against unjust abortion policies and wage disparities for women are examples. Many of these leaders are in churches. However, some of these leaders emerge on the periphery of churches and faith institutions; even still many of these Agents of Compassion and Justice retain an abiding faith in God. Though enlisting minorities for leadership will work, that plan cannot be the sole source of finding Agents of Compassion and Justice. For this nation to truly be changed, Agents of Compassion and Justice will have to rise up inside and outside of churches, in minority and majority groups—in every walk of life.

SEARCHING FOR AGENTS OF COMPASSION AND JUSTICE THROUGH JESUS' EXAMPLE

How else do we locate Agents of Compassion and Justice? We find them through modeling Jesus' example to show compassion for those who are marginalized:

> Then Jesus went about all the cities and villages, teaching in their synagogues, and proclaiming the good news of the kingdom, and curing every disease and every sickness. When he saw the crowds, he had compassion for them, because they were harassed and helpless, like sheep without a shepherd. Then he said to his disciples, "The harvest is plentiful, but the laborers are few; therefore ask the Lord of the harvest to send out laborers into his harvest." (Matt. 9:35–38)

Jesus faced a society that was filled with sickness and disease. Further, the people coming to him for help were harassed and helpless—like unprotected sheep. The crime is that these people should have been protected because they were Jews under the supervision of priests in the synagogues. Though leadership was in place for them, they found themselves as victims of the ravages of life. Recognizing the lack of care and concern for those diseased, harassed, and helpless, Jesus shows compassion. We may locate the Agents of Compassion and Justice in our day by acknowledging those who stand alongside the marginalized and offer care and concern.

In this Scripture, Jesus—an Agent of Compassion and Justice—instructs his disciples to pray with a simple request: send laborers!

As we continue to follow Jesus' example, to find Agents of Compassion and Justice, we must pray. We must create environments for connecting to God with the sole purpose of locating those who work on God's behalf to create a better society. You may question if the title was changed from Apostle to Agent to include those beyond the bounds of church, why then would the action of prayer be involved? Prayer, unlike the word "apostle," finds itself at home in many places outside the church walls. Taking time to talk to God—to get quiet—to calm our spirits—to invoke God's presence—are all necessary disciplines to discern where to locate and connect with leaders dedicated to building compassionate and just communities. These disciplines of the spirit certainly exist in corridors beyond church walls.

This Scripture provides yet another template of Agents of Compassion and Justice. Note that prayer follows the work of compassion and justice. Jesus and the disciples went into the cities and villages and did the work of curing diseases and showing compassion. Then, he directed them to pray. *As Agents of Compassion and Justice, our prayers will have more potency after we have done the work of compassion and justice ourselves.* While we work, "a sense of what is vital" grows within us, which enables us to identify a sense of what is vital in another.[17]

Of equal note, Jesus did not just *do* the work of healing; he also displayed compassion. He created an environment of love and understanding. Jesus had empathy. He could see that they were harassed and helpless. By creating a community of love and understanding, Jesus gives a template on how to identify Agents of Compassion and Justice. They are those who don't just do work, but they show care and build connection with those in need. So, too, does Thurman highlight this need for belonging and understanding:

It may not be far-fetched to examine a [person's] need to be loved, to be understood, to be cared for as the essential building blocks for the actualizing of his [or her] potential and the essential stuff of community among [people]. . . . There is an insistent connection between the need for well-being and the elemental necessity in all forms of life to actualize its own potential and thus fulfill itself.[18]

Thurman asserts that caring for someone helps that person realize his or her own potential. When a person is nurtured, the person is better able to find his or her own way in life. When we engage in the work as Apostles of Sensitiveness or Agents of Compassion and Justice, we free those we care for to follow God's will for their lives. "As we're liberated from our own fear, Our presence automatically liberates others."[19]

Doing the work of an Agent of Compassion and Justice ignites the fire in other Agents who have yet to be revealed. That work takes away the barriers that prevent others from identifying themselves as Agents. Suffering from racism, sexism, trafficking, heterosexism, homophobia, or a destructive culture of war can so preoccupy people's focus that they will not have the time or stamina to ascertain their life's path. However, when persons are relieved from their suffering by an Agent, they receive a new breath and have the space to discern their life's purpose.

MEDITATION AS A DISCIPLINE TO SUSTAIN AGENTS OF COMPASSION AND JUSTICE

Far too many activists, pastors, and change agents are sidelined by justice fatigue. Meditation is a way of sustaining Agents of Compassion and Justice, as is prayer. Meditation is a discipline of quieting the spirit and focusing the mind in a particular direction or on a specific topic. Thurman believes that this activity is one of renewal, especially for those dealing with national issues. Thurman says that, in cases where the Apostle is not victorious in his or her quest, he or she can still survive through maintaining the practice of meditation.[20] Meditation centers and grounds the Agent—especially in times of sorrow or defeat—so that she or he may process the previous encounter and discover strength within to continue the work of compassion and justice.

The act of meditation does not just sustain agents; it also does the direct work of identifying them. Thurman denotes a difference between fate and destiny. "Fate is the raw material of experience. . . . Destiny is what a man [or woman] does with these raw materials."[21] He then proffers that meditation or reflection on one's fate helps one to ascertain destiny:

> Out of this contact we build destiny. We determine what we shall do with our circumstances. It is here that religion makes one of its most important contributions to life. It is a resource that provides

strength, stability and confidence as one works at one's destiny. It gives assurance of a God who shares in the issue and whose everlasting arms are always there.[22]

By encouraging persons to meditate on what is happening in their lives and how they need to respond, those very persons can construct their destiny as they get strength and restoration. Thurman asserts that this strength comes from a supportive and present God. Therefore, by creating an environment of meditation and searching, Agents can be born as well as sustained. Current Agents of Compassion and Justice must form communities of meditation and searching for all persons to assist in forming Agents for the future.

CONCLUSION

Seventy-five years after Rev. Dr. Howard Thurman became a part of the pastoral leadership of Fellowship Church and began to call forth Apostles of Sensitiveness to fight the social ills of his time, this country finds itself in kindred circumstances. We, too, must call forth those who will fight the ills of our time—who will battle the New Jim Crow, who will fight for the rights of the disenfranchised, who will speak truth to power. We must enlist Agents of Compassion and Justice through prayer, love, and meditation. The hope is that they will revolutionize our nation, improve our ability to form loving community, and encourage justice for all. However, their success is not based on any particular outcome; rather, their success is determined by the faithfulness of their journey. Regardless of the outcome, the Agent of Compassion and Justice will have joy. Such joy doesn't derive from a triumph or an accomplished feat; instead, it comes from the knowledge that God is with the Agent as a Companion at all times.[23]

GROUNDING QUESTIONS

1. Who are the Apostles of Sensitiveness in the United States? How can they heal generational woes and untreated national wounds?
2. What is the relationship between compassionate justice work and prayer?
3. How might meditation sustain you and prevent justice fatigue?

10

When the Magic Happens
I Struggle to Catch My Breath

Planting Seeds of Community
on Common Ground

TYLER HO-YIN SIT

God is present with me this day. God is present with me in the midst of my anxieties. . . . Little by little, I am beginning to understand that deliverance from anxiety means fundamental growth in spiritual character and awareness. It becomes a quality of being, emerging from deep within, giving to all the dimensions of experience a vast immunity against being anxious. A ground of calm underlies experiences whatever may be the tempestuous character of events. This calm is the manifestation in life of the active, dynamic Presence of God. . . .

I seek new levels of awareness of the meaning of the commonplace. It is easy for me to take things for granted and to deal with them without sensitiveness. When have you noticed the color in the sky? When have you looked at the shape and place of a tree? What about the light in the eyes of your friend when she smiles? There's magic all around us. In the rocks and trees, and in the minds of humans. Deep hidden springs of magic.

—Howard Thurman, *Meditations of the Heart*[1]

GOD IS PRESENT

The Tsuglagkhang, the big temple next to the residence of the Dalai Lama, is so clean it shines. Fresh white walls make cuts of flowers pop, especially as they adorn ancient statues of Guru Rinpoche and the goddess Tara. Monks in their distinctive scarlet robes, humble and clean, amble throughout the grounds. The lay Tibetans pass by prayer wheels, spinning them with their hands. On the days that the Dalai Lama does appear, like if he's returning from a trip, the whole town (whether Tibetan or a foreigner like me) lines the streets and greets the motorcade going by. For six months I observed this tradition as an outsider who was received with great hospitality. The Tibetans fed me fried dough for the Losar holiday; introduced me to Tibetan philosophy; and, on one sunny day, I met His Holiness the Dalai Lama.

155

The small group of North Americans in my program put on our best clothes and fumbled through the notecards that held our most profound-sounding questions scribbled in the margins. We walked down vast white halls and passed through extensive security checks; one body guard per attendee, I observed. The tight level of security juxtaposed the bright, airy room in which we sat. We fidgeted in our chairs. My eyes roamed, and even in the sunlight I could barely see even one speck of dust. Then he entered. He strolled into our room with the same feet that had walked through the Himalayan mountains to find sanctuary for his people. He looked at us students with gentle eyes, eyes that amazingly were unhardened after all the violence and chaos he had witnessed. This spiritual and political leader of the Tibetans moved with grace, laughed heartily, and sat down with us in his crimson robes. I traced the curve of his shaved head with my eyes, and wondered, How am I so close to this man right now? How is someone who has dedicated untold hours to sacred learning sitting in arm's reach of me? The scene was so beautiful, I struggled to catch my breath.

Four years later . . .

With each efforted exhale, he breathed a warm alcohol-laden breath across my uncovered arm. Droplets of sweat ran down his neck and disappeared into his faded red shirt. The intoxicated man slept in fits and bursts on my shoulder. As the city bus maneuvered around potholes and speed bumps, his head dozed and snapped back up. "Thank you so much," he blurted out when I switched seats with him so he could lean against the window (and not on me). The red-shirted man continued, "I'm so sorry. Sometimes I drink until I black out, then I wake up and I'm still drunk. . . . I'm on my way to an AA meeting with my friend." He nodded to a yellow-shirted woman scrolling on her phone from the bus's back row. It looked like she didn't have an easy night either. "I'm so sorry," he muttered once more before falling asleep.

If Howard Thurman's meditation is true, I encountered God in the company of the Dalai Lama—with his legion of devotees—and in the presence of the red-shirted man on the city bus. Thurman insisted that the Spirit of God is within everyone, no matter what kind of day they had, no matter how many hours they've spent on a prayer mat, no matter who they have betrayed. The Spirit of God is just as available as the next breath, whether that's a deep breath of practiced contemplation or a harried breath drifting in and out of consciousness. Drawing upon Thurman's wisdom and a series of personal anecdotes as a church planter, this chapter examines the overarching presence of God in the lives of those we encounter and the "deep hidden springs of magic" of the world in which we live.

DEEP HIDDEN SPRINGS

Years ago, as a kid, I stood for the first time on the banks of the mighty Mississippi River. Completely in awe, I marveled at the surging black water that would travel another thousand miles downstream. Stretching my childhood mind, I asked my parents, "Does the river ever take a break? Does the water ever stop?" They looked at me thoughtfully and replied: "The river is always flowing." That's how the Spirit of God is. Always flowing, always there.

I trust Thurman on strategies to overcome discrimination and build community, as he cultivated a garden of spirituality in the wasteland of a struggle. No stranger to hardship, Thurman was the grandson of a former slave, who was born and raised in a poor racially segregated community. During his seminary years in upstate New York, he spoke of the perils of racism before well-intentioned whites and ornery Ku Klux Klan members. In the mid-1940s, he broke barriers by cofounding an interracial church in San Francisco, perhaps the first church of its kind in the United States. Thurman continued this work of building beloved community, at my alma mater, Boston University, where he served as the first African American Dean of Marsh Chapel and welcomed people of different faiths and cultural backgrounds to worship. Thurman knew the fires of struggle and, through them, refined a deep empathy that allowed him to be in ministry with an incredible diversity of people. Through those brown, empathetic eyes, Thurman could see deep hidden springs in unlikely faces, and that's why people flocked to him. There is nothing the soul longs for more than to be recognized for what it is.

Two decades after his departure from Boston University, the institution founded the Howard Thurman Center for Common Ground. Through cultural-based programs, lectures, and events, this center aims to "spread Thurman's belief in the unity of all people." During my student days, The Thurman Center served as a site for students of different backgrounds to meet, debate, face adversities together, and dream. As a young gay man with aspirations to ordained ministry, the center bearing Thurman's name inspired me to envision a world where true inclusivity was actually possible. We came to the center to bare our anxieties, and it was between those walls that we discovered the Spirit of God showing up because of, not despite, those fears.

One spot in the center is particularly inspired. Campus tour guides refer to this area as a "serpentine glass wall," a smooth glass wall that winds back and forth between meeting rooms and the large gathering space. The inward and outward curves symbolize the inward and outward journey of life. That glass wall reminded me of the significance of looking inside as a means to change the world around me. Rather than pursuing a type of spirituality that results in a detachment from my surrounding, this magical glass emboldened me to spiral people *out* into the world and seek connection with all who fall under the presence of God's light. In the wisdom of that glass wall, I uncovered a key to planting churches begins by shining light on my inner world and then radiating outward into community. Below, I outline three central practices pivotal to church planting.

SACRED WITNESSING: STORY SHARING AS A PATH TO COMMUNITY BUILDING

Not long ago, a young woman in my church taught me the relationship between story sharing and community building. On that day, she shared with me the heartache of dating an alcoholic. She explained, "The alcohol, which is so common in everyday American life, took on new power. Inside of each bottle wasn't just liquid but a hurricane: the frustration of emotional detachment, the uncertainty of how the night would go, the embarrassment of dashed expectations." But her relationship was far from cinematic drama; she described it as "a slow drift into loneliness while sharing a life with someone who was imploding." The woman confessed to me that she withheld the worst stories from her loved ones to protect her partner. However, her life changed when her partner skipped her birthday to get drunk. As a gift to herself, she attended her first meeting of Al-Anon, a group for the loved ones of alcoholics. The gathering was in an unremarkable church basement with folding chairs and the like. Someone handed her a book with a creased cover, then they read aloud. Next, they opened the floor for each person in the circle to speak if they felt called to do so. Each shared a story. She almost fell out of her folding chair, when she came to the realization, "I never realized how alone I was. The simple power of telling people my story and *seeing* others share their stories freed me."

From the encounter with the freed woman, I recognized that disclosing a deep-down truth illumines a hopeful path for meaningful connection. Even though sharing your story with others induces anxieties, of which Thurman speaks, it is in that same company that unprecedented spiritual growth and awareness are possible. This is the fine art of what we at New City, the United Methodist church I planted in Minneapolis, Minnesota, started calling "sacred witnessing."

Sacred witnessing moves beyond superficially acknowledging suffering, hardship, or difference. Seeing through a sacred lens recognizes God's presence in your life and seeks to see the Divine in other people. In this regard witnessing is a prayerful act that draws the seer into viewing self, other, and the earth with compassion and care. From this vantage the world becomes filled with divine appearances, and even the most perilous situations can become an eye test for holiness.

DISCOVERING COMMON GROUND:
PATIENT GENERATIONAL HEALING

Sacred witnessing, which values the divinity and humanity in all persons, provides the foundation for discovering "common ground." On such ground, the widest chasms can be crossed for relationship building. However, far too often, people, especially those with dominant identities (like male, white, able-bodied, etc.) attempt to shortcut the process of relationship building by offering reductionistic statements like "I don't see color," or "It doesn't matter what color you are, black, white, or purple." Not only does colorblindness negate the opportunity to see the uniqueness of the individual, it also diminishes the potential richness of community to be formed.

Feel-good affirmations or trite statements to relieve guilt rarely achieve common ground. Common ground is developed through cultivating practices of rich belonging. It takes time. Shortly after launching our ministry, a member in our congregation offered a lesson on the patience needed to foster rich belonging. This member is a refugee from Southeast Asia who had moved to Minnesota. While we both were of Asian descent, this member who had been displaced from U.S. foreign policy, reflected on home, nation, and time differently than me. In referencing these matters, she shared, "My grandmother, mother, and I have all been refugees. With God as my witness, my child will have a home and stay there." Rich belonging is the consequence of intentionality, sacrifice, and healing that takes generations. Such healing and belonging does not come after attending one workshop, reading a dozen self-help books, or visiting church a hundred times.

But the Spirit doesn't mind. She's not in a hurry. She's been doing her work before colonization, before the rise and fall of empires, before tanks or chariots, before the Tower of Babel, before Adam and Eve ate fruit, before leaves, before rain, before booming stars, before the black stretches of space even started. The Spirit is more patient, and more persistent, than any of us. She has been bending the moral arc of the universe toward justice with her strong hands, whether it was despite or because of us. And she's alive in *us*, in our bodies.

MOVING BEYOND RADICAL DIFFERENCE BY HOLDING INCOMPATIBLE TRUTHS

During my first year of seminary, I was a prison chaplain in a detention center in Atlanta. In the corner cell was a man who I was socialized to find disgusting. I am a self-proclaimed progressive, Asian, midwesterner. He was a self-proclaimed southern bigot. His opinions about gay people did not break any stereotypes, and, perhaps, outside of these circumstances, he may have found me repulsive as well. However, he was a terminally ill inmate, and I was the chaplain tasked with offering him care.

Due to a medical condition, the southerner's liver was functionally replaced by an external bag that had to be switched out by a nurse. At times, the bag dripped a sickly yellow bile on his prison sheets. The smell was enough to knock many back to the hallway.

The southerner never disclosed why he was in prison, but through whispers I pieced together that he was incarcerated for a sex crime that likely involved children. Media-socialized stereotypes told me that I should not be in that corner cell with him. Internal whispers warned that people like me have been hurt by men like this. My academic training of historical ideologies and social systems echoed narratives of bigoted southern white men who have long oppressed others. Across the gamut of reasons, my whole body told me to not go into that cell. I could visit with the cancer patients and the dying, with the dealers and the guys who started fights, but my instincts rebelled against me going into that corner cell. And yet, he kept coming up in my prayers. As if ANCHORED in a current, I was moved to offer pastoral support despite myself. It became the greatest test of sacred witnessing I would face yet—given our differences, would we be able to experience the divine in community with each other?

As I pondered how to connect with this man so different than me, I imagined the types of conversations Thurman held with not-so-well-intentioned members of the Boston University campus when he became the first Black dean of Marsh Chapel. Or with people who doubted his church planting in San Francisco. If Thurman could cross those chasms not merely with reluctance but with prayerful joy and vigor, I reasoned, then I could too. If Thurman could find the Spirit back then in a strange land, then I could find the Spirit right now in unfamiliar company. So, I did what my tradition trained me to do: I prayed not only for myself but also for the one who seemed to oppose me.

Covered in prayer, the first time I stepped into the corner cell, I pushed through the smell and sought to see the sacred in one I deemed much different. He nodded to me as I entered. I knew that finding common ground and rich belonging would take time, so I was undeterred when the conversation started off slow. I had to lean in, almost falling on to his bed, because of his speech pattern. Part of this inmate's tongue was surgically removed and affected his speech. Moreover, our accents clashed as my midwestern dialect and his southern twang mixed like oil and vinegar. Yet through our differences we endured.

On some days we read the Psalms together, while on others we sat and watched *Wheel of Fortune*. I recall that in those early days he tried to coerce me to breach protocol by lending him a pen or by sending a letter on his behalf. From my training, I identified these as power plays, and I set appropriate boundaries. As our parameters clarified, day by day, he eventually opened up. One day, he mentioned that no one else in the prison had spoken one word to him the entire week. Lacking meaningful encounters with others, the southern man described his term as solitary confinement even though people were physically around him. He confessed that when his term began, he received letters from family; but as the years wore on the letters stopped. That year for Thanksgiving, I put together a worship service, which he attended. I'll never forget him standing in the back and weeping as we sang "Amazing Grace." The scene was so beautiful, I struggled to catch my breath.

When my chest stopped heaving and I could duly reflect on this redemption story, I learned that ministry in complex situations involves holding two, seemingly incompatible truths at the same time:

— Oppressed people and oppressing people have radically different lives
— God made us all family

The capacity to hold both of these, deeply, is a sweet fruit of spiritual practice. After my encounter with the detained southern man, I can now look at someone who is "the kind of person who oppresses people like me" and still see deep hidden wells.

Clinging to these tensions became more challenging on the chilly winter day when news rolled through Atlanta that Trayvon Martin died. Just one state away the seventeen-year-old African American male Martin was gunned down by a volunteer neighborhood watchman named George Zimmerman who sought to "stand his ground." As the news thundered through the prison, inmates started to share long-buried stories. In their presence, I heard of African American fathers giving "the talk" to their children on how to respond to law enforcement and other authorities and not get shot. Here I am an Asian man welcomed into the confidence of Black fathers, and challenged, once again, to hold incompatible truths. But as a church planter, I have learned my job is not to have all the answers or even bring life from the seed. My job is to prepare the ground and invite the seed into a relationship with the only One who can deepen roots and make life spring forth.

THE PLANTER'S PARADOX

As a church planter, I embrace the challenge of planting seeds that only God can nourish. Still, I seek to till the soil and blaze trails for rich belonging through the practice of sacred witnessing. I scatter seeds with full knowledge that generational healing takes time. Even still, I dirty my hands in the work of community across difference, as I hold incompatible truths and pray for God's amazing grace.

Here lies the challenge for people who believe in justice. Our task is to bridge unlikely relationships with people who are radically different than us—for when we do, we witness God's presence and the deep Spirit springs of creation all around us. It's a miracle, truly, and not one to be minimized.

I conclude with a brief reflection on the planter's paradox of drawing together the simultaneous need for relational and systemic transformation without letting one diminish the other. In his dynamic sermon "Men Who've Walked with God," Thurman negotiates the space between building beloved community and challenging systems of power. To frame this argument he reflects on the Essene community, a Jewish sect contemporaneous with Jesus:

> [The Essenes] withdrew from cutting a Roman's neck off or doing a lot of other things out here, but they were not withdrawing from the struggle. They felt that the way to do it is to move underneath the foundation that stabilizes the evil order. And if you move at that level . . . everything that is above you will begin to crumble and fall. Because there is no power less than the power of God that is capable of withstanding the power of God. Therefore, if I can release as a living channel, the living energy of God into the situation, anything that is less than that that is in the situation will be destroyed. That is what a mystic does with social action. He [she] is no coward, sticking his [her] head in the sand, praying to God because he's [she's] scared or because he [she] doesn't have the nerve to do anything else. But he [she] is sure that he [she] is in touch with terrible energy, terrible energy. And, if his [her] life can be a point of focus through which that energy hits its mark in the world, then the redemptive process can work. And that is why the way of the mystic is so difficult, and yet in some ways so simple.[2]

Like the mystical Essenes, as a church planter, I have learned to move where the edges fray between "solitude" and "community," and where "relationships" and "systems" overlap. God wants to work with all of it. God wants all of it to bend toward justice, toward *shalom*. From Thurman's conception of the mystic, I draw a vision for church planters who dig irrigation paths for the ceaseless river of God to flow through until no corner of the earth is parched by evil. To the prison, planters must go, then to the courts and schools. From churches to main streets, we flow with a God who demands not perfection but intimacy, not a mighty chorus but the sound of the genuine. This kind of planter strains to hear divinity echoing within themselves, then in other people, then the whole world. Further, we must wail on everything that obstructs that voice in ourselves, in other people, and in the world.

In the still of the evening, when the sun has gone down and the frogs croak louder than the traffic on the street, I revel in all the sacred encounters I have witnessed in my life. Whether it be the caring eyes of His Holiness Dali Lama or the stuttering of the sleeping man on the city bus, God is there. In the sacred storytelling of the woman at Al-Anon and the Southeast Asian refugee who longs for generational freedom, God is there. In the midst of our anxieties, God flows freely in the self-proclaimed southern bigot and the incarcerated African American father, each entrusting a story and holding seemingly incompatible truths. "All around us worlds are dying and worlds are being born." We are the planters commissioned to lay down, gently, the worlds that are dying, and watch with expectation the worlds being born.

GROUNDING QUESTIONS

1. Remember a moment in your life when you formed an unlikely friendship. How did you see the sacred in the person so different from you?
2. In a culture that moves at breakneck speed, how can you create a space for generational healing to unfold?
3. How can people who do not agree with each other stay in relationship while challenging harmful beliefs?
4. What incompatible truths must you hold to build community in your family, your neighborhood, your school, or your job?

Conclusion

Embracing the Quest

LUTHER E. SMITH JR.

A DEEP AND INSATIABLE HUNGER

At the closing banquet of the 1972 National Committee of Black Churchmen Conference, I was eager to hear the featured speaker: Howard Thurman. This would be my first time to hear this preacher who had inspired so many I knew. And since Thurman was chosen for this climax event, I anticipated a thunderous delivery of a message that would be a tribute to the black church's role in overcoming racial oppression.

Howard Thurman's delivery was not thunderous. His message about the black church was as much challenge as tribute. And rather than stressing how to mobilize black churchgoers to combat systems of injustice, he spoke to the significance in the struggle for justice of attending to the inner life. Thurman and his address were 180 degrees from what I expected. I left the banquet hall astonished and inspired. In my hotel room I felt wholly and holy lost in the bliss of oneness. I knew that what he said and what I was feeling resonated with my deep and insatiable hunger, and that all my coming days would be informed by what I had just experienced.

I believe what Thurman had awakened in me is similar to his impact upon all this book's writers. Whether early or later in our careers, Thurman made a connection that led us to experience him as a companion for life's journey. The types of connection may vary—his focus on

Jesus' identity and liberating message to the disinherited; the significance of religious experience to faith; the primacy of community to our
personal and collective formation; his explication of sacred texts; the
importance of attending to one's personal spiritual life for the sake of
self and one's availability to social transformation; the beatific vision of
loving relationships that include and extend beyond our racial, ethnic,
gender, and cultural identities; these and many other guiding lessons
have animated the writing of this book.

All of us speak of his ideas and witness that inspire our embrace
of him. Still, we are drawn to Thurman by something more than his
insights on particular subjects. His way of engaging the life quest *with
head and heart* guides us to recognize and respond to a deep and insatiable hunger within. The hunger is felt in our various passions for pursuing justice, discerning biblical authority, healing personal and social
trauma, and affirming identity. The hunger motivates us to pursue our
passions. But the hunger is not synonymous with our passions. The
hunger is a driving force in the quest for meaning and fulfillment. Any
effort to eliminate the hunger is misguided. The hunger is to be cherished and sustained by being fed.

My experience of Thurman at the 1972 conference mirrors Howard Thurman's transformational experience as a high school student.
While attending a YMCA student conference in North Carolina, he
heard Mordecai Johnson preach in a vesper service. Reflecting on the
impact of Johnson's sermon, forty-four years later Thurman says,

> I don't know what he talked about now; I don't know what he said.
> But as I listened to him, I knew what would be the area and the
> meaning of my life quest. I did not know in terms of a bill of par-
> ticulars. I could not spell it out in terms of precise goals. But I knew
> more deeply than I understood. . . . But it was years after before the
> feeling I sensed that night worked itself up into the region of my
> deliberations of my feelings and my choosings.[1]

Mordecai Johnson's sermon had engaged Thurman's deep hunger. The
implications from being awakened anew to the hunger were not immediately known. However, living to respond faithfully to the hunger
became Thurman's vocation.

I perceived Thurman to be a mentor for the hunger I felt. I knew
that my own sense of vocation aligned with what I felt from his spirit
and message at the conference. After a year of reading his books and
speaking with others about him, I wrote Thurman to ask if I might visit

with him at his home in San Francisco. I indicated that I had no agenda except honoring what I sensed to be a compelling desire of my spirit to connect with him. I mentioned that perhaps my request was analogous to his desire to meet with the Quaker mystic Rufus Jones after reading Jones's book *Finding the Trail of Life*.[2] Thurman agreed to the meeting and extended a full day for us to be in conversation. Before I ever considered Thurman to be a subject of my scholarship, this was the beginning of our relationship—an intimate time of personal disclosures that entrusted heart with heart.

The hunger of the spirit seeks companionship. In addition to pivotal teachers and his grandmother, Thurman sought Mordecai Johnson and Rufus Jones as companions to instruct him on the quest.[3] Although the hunger is personal, the necessary response to the hunger is relational.

The hunger of the spirit seeks. Pursuing fulfillment involves searching, asking, reflecting, endeavoring to discover, questing.[4] The centrality of questing to living a vital life in a complex and dynamic world is evident in Thurman:

> The possibility of quest, the miracle of being able to seek, is rooted, it seems to me, in the very nature of life. . . . The possibility of seeking, the possibility of bringing to bear upon a goal the resources of the personality so that as the individual begins to actualize his [her] potential and becomes himself [herself] more and more the living embodiment of that for which he's [she's] questing, [requires perceiving the reality of life as fluid and creative].[5]

Some of the destinations for Thurman's questing are found in the chapter titles of two of his books. In *Deep Is the Hunger*, the seeking occurs in "A Sense of History," "A Sense of Self," "A Sense of Presence [God]," and in "The Quiet Times." In *The Search for Common Ground*, the chapter titles convey a similar seeking—"The Search into Beginnings [creation myths]," "The Search in Living Structures [biological functioning]," "The Search in the Prophet's Dream [utopian and religious visions]," "The Search in the Common Consciousness [between humans and other animals]," and "The Search in Identity [personal and collective]"—that provide clues to the dreams, fundamentals, and challenges for becoming community. In addition to these titles, Thurman's writing and speaking seek meaning in sacred Scriptures and his personal experiences.

I always felt that Thurman's companionship on my quest entailed a broad and rich appreciation for the wonder and enormous complexity of life. His counsel did not avoid the perplexing issues of faith, human behavior, and scientific inquiry. At times, ongoing questions, silence, confusion, and frustration were the most authentic responses he could offer. I could relax my urge to have solutions when what I most needed was to appreciate the difficulty in discerning what is true.

His appreciation for complexity and humility in the questing process was not based on a belief that truth can only be interpreted through relativism. Thurman was deeply convicted about the common ground for truth, justice, love, and ultimate meaning. He writes, "I believe, with my forefathers, that this is God's world. This faith has had to fight against disillusionment, despair, and the vicissitudes of American history."[6] Thurman often said, "God bottoms existence." The experiences of God and understandings of the experiences are personal. Therefore, interpretations of the experiences are varied and influenced by factors of personal history and culture. Still, God is the ultimate reality, whether acknowledged or ignored, for all that is rightly discerned to be true:

> The goal of life is God! The source of life is God! That out of which life comes is that into which life goes. [God] out of whom life comes is [God] into whom life goes. God is the goal of man's [woman's] life, the end of all his [her] seeking, the meaning of all his [her] striving. God is the guarantor of all his [her] values, the ultimate meaning—the timeless frame of reference.[7]

The deep and insatiable hunger may be perceived and named in a thousand different ways. Those who study and pray and argue fervently often come to conclusions that are at odds with others whose lives have been devoted to fervent study, prayer, and argument. The conflicts have resulted in outcomes of friendly coexistence and deadly combat. Questing to satisfy the hunger can be a matter of life and death. Unfortunately, too often devotion to the God who "bottoms" and loves all of us is sacrificed to maligning and ostracizing (in the name of God) those who believe otherwise.

Howard Thurman's focus on the deep hunger for God's dream embraces differences in beliefs and practices. I think of Thurman as a "big tent" spiritual guide. After meeting Thurman on one's journey, one frequently connects with others whose experience of reading or listening to Thurman has led them on a path to the big tent where hospitality and creative fellowship are extended to all. In the tent, I have experienced Pentecostals, Episcopalians, Quakers, Presbyterians,

Baptists, Methodists, Unitarian/Universalists, Roman Catholics, Buddhists, Muslims, Hindus, agnostics, and many other people of faith who acknowledge Thurman as a guiding resource for their being in the big tent gathering. The distinctive theologies do not disappear. Still, partaking in the experience of communion with one another feeds the deep hunger.

Thurman does not provide a detailed map that guarantees arrival with the insights, practices, people, and institutions that satisfy the hunger. The myriad complexities and uncertainties of belief systems and believers cannot be charted. The risk of being misguided is pervasive. And the anxiety that all this uncertainty fosters is unnerving. For many, the risk and anxiety are so threatening that retreat to citadels of orthodoxy and like-minded believers becomes the road most traveled.

Thurman's spirituality does not deny the unsettling power of uncertainty. The quest, however, has a certainty that is sufficient to engage all risks. That certainty is God.

The certainty goes beyond assurance of God's abiding presence in the journey. Thurman asserts the certainty that God will provide the needed response to the hunger that motivates the quest: he says, "When a man [woman] quests and in his [her] quest he [she] honors a deep and insatiable hunger of his [her] spirit, and in response to that hunger he [she] more and more begins to feed it with all the raw materials of his [her] stuff, then the hunger has to be honored by life, and I think by God."[8]

This is a rare obligatory outcome of the spiritual quest that Thurman professes. I suspect that it comes from Rufus Jones mentoring Thurman on the spirituality of the thirteenth- and fourteenth-century mystic, Meister Eckhart. Eckhart repeatedly insists that God *must* respond to persons who ardently give themselves to fulfilling the hunger:

> You must know that God is bound to act, to pour [God's self] out into you as soon as ever [God] finds you ready. . . . When [God] finds you ready, [God] is obligated to act, to flow into you, just as the sun must shine out and is unable to stop itself whenever the air is bright and clear. It would be a very grave defect indeed in God if, finding you so empty and so bare, [God] did not do any excellent work in you and did not fill you with glorious gifts.[9]

The companionship dimension to questing is evident here. Eckhart is a companion to Jones and Thurman on their quests. His declaration tutors Thurman's declaration that the deep and insatiable hunger *will be fed by God* when accompanied by the work of preparation and readiness. In God our questing has a reliable ANCHOR for the journey into uncertain currents.

I WILL SING A NEW SONG

During my first visit with Howard Thurman, I had a sense of surprise as he spoke. I felt the surprise, but I could not name it. Later that day the confusion broke, and I wrote that he has "a spirit of eternal youth." At age seventy-five he spoke with excitement about current events and the implications they had for understanding the quest. Despite the pressing demands on his time, he wanted to restart practicing the clarinet and painting. Only four years earlier he published *The Search for Common Ground,* which examined biological and social science research and contemporary struggles for identity in his quest to perceive structures of unity in life. In his home he told me many stories about his life; yet I did not feel that we were lingering in the past. The animated conversations on this first and subsequent visits were directed to present and coming realities.

Thurman's vitality for seeking sustains his belief that growth and transformation are essential to the questing demands of faith. In his book *Disciplines of the Spirit,* growth is one of five major disciplines that prepare us for the creative encounter with God. Growth entails more than becoming wiser through experience. Growth involves being transformed in ways that result in one's life being increasingly "centered" on the experience of God. He writes, "It is small wonder that so much is made in the Christian religion of the necessity of rebirths. There need not be only one single rebirth, but again and again a man [woman] may be reborn until at last there is nothing that remains between him [her] and God."[10]

Growth enables us to perceive ourselves as becoming. We are neither defined nor held captive by our past. The discipline of growth liberates us from the crushing impact of failures and misdeeds. We can live in the present and prepare to move into the future with readiness and a fresh spirit for encountering life and God.

Thurman's meditation, "I Will Sing a New Song," expresses this conviction. Singing a new song involves not only becoming more alive to life and God, it requires becoming more alive to myself. I must take seriously that the quest is taken into the interior landscape of my mind, emotions, and spirit. I should not enlist on a journey under the assumption that all the important encounters and discoveries are external to who I am and who I understand myself to be. Failing to recognize this underestimates the challenges to be faced and overestimates my capacity to quest successfully.

After speaking at a college about Howard Thurman's emphasis on engaging the self, a student approached me and said: "Recently, my professor told the class that he didn't understand all the talk about finding one's self. He said, 'if you want to find yourself, just look in the mirror.'" As he told this incident, the student's expression indicated confusion over what he had just heard from me and what the professor had declared to be a waste of time. Unfortunately, this educator gave a terrible answer to students who hungered for insight about their quest. The self is complex and vast. Like the quest into nature and human nature, exploring and discovering the self is never exhausted.

On a visit to Thurman's home, I arrived during a period when he was listening to recordings of his sermons and lectures from over the decades of his ministry. A staff member of the Howard Thurman Educational Trust was present and working to catalog the recordings by subject matter. Watching Thurman as we listened, his face and hands were very animated in response to what he heard. Most often it was difficult to know if he felt positively or negatively about what he was hearing. However, at times his face would lift, a smile would come forth, the hands punctuated the air, a deep breath was drawn, and it was clear that something had resonated deeply with his spirit. When one of the recordings finished, he relaxed and said, "This whole process of listening to myself has been a very emotional time. Sometimes I listen and lament that I had the nerve to preach. At other times a word comes through that instructs me on this journey."

Howard Thurman listened to Howard Thurman. Howard Thurman was instructed and guided on his quest by Howard Thurman. Guidance comes from within, and we are foolish, or at least impoverished, to ignore this invaluable resource for the quest. Our desire to live creatively in our environments is dependent upon valuing our selves and our capacities to be reliable sources for discernment and understanding. Thurman counsels with the question, "How can one believe that life has meaning, if his [her] own life does not have meaning?"[11] Thurman restates this sentiment when he frequently quotes from Rabindranath Tagore's translation of *Songs of Kabir*: "Here is the truth! Go where you will, to Benares or to Mathura; if you do not find your soul, the world is unreal to you."[12] As mentioned previously, feeding the deep hunger involves engaging a sense of self.

Thurman's emphasis on seeking the meaning of one's self and the conditions of one's inner landscape has been pivotal to my spiritual formation. My earliest memories of childhood recall the high value that family and church stressed on honoring every person's worth—including my own. I feel deeply indebted to this instruction and love. This is the fertile soil in which Thurman's lessons have taken root in me.

His instruction has not only been helpful for cultivating my sense of self; it has also been wise counsel for discerning how social transformation efforts are best sustained. I have lived through periods where protest leaders indoctrinated followers by asserting that the goals of the protest movement were the supreme value. Individuals' significance was measured by the extent they advanced the goals of the movement. Using a chess analogy, individuals were pawns that could be quickly sacrificed to achieve a victory. Devotion was declared for the oppressed masses, while the treatment of individuals within the organization could be manipulative and abusive.

As an activist and observer, I witnessed at least two defeating outcomes from the "personal significance does not count" approach. One, it strips away an individual's basic need to be understood, loved, and honored. Members eventually experience this stripping as a loss of energy and commitment to the cause. Members leaving a movement is one of the diminishing results. Dysfunctional conflicts among those who remain are another. And two, being active and successful in a struggle for justice involves tenacity that is fueled by self-awareness, affirmation, and hope. Articulated or not, the question "Who am I?" must be answered with a response that does not just refer to the importance of the cause. Stirring within us is the need to know ourselves sufficiently as persons of infinite worth. Who am I when the cause is not successful? Who am I when I'm not involved in the cause? Who am I when my contributions to a movement are demeaned? If left unattended, these questions can haunt and wreak havoc on the spirit and mental health of those who remain involved.

As with the college professor mentioned above and some social activists, introspection has too often been characterized as self-indulgent. The pejorative term "navel gazing" is used to depict an individual whose attention to self leaves the person oblivious to the surrounding reality. Self-awareness has mistakenly been made synonymous with selfishness. But what are the dangers in becoming a stranger to one's self? How might the failure to attend to one's own emotional landscape disable a person's ability to connect with another's emotional landscape? My testimony is that being centered (self aware) in myself is crucial to being centered in life. My interaction with family, friends, vocation, social causes, nature, and strangers is informed by the state of my interior life. I must be aware of the convictions and feelings that inhabit my interior life if I hope to live creatively with all of life.

In the previous section I wrote that embracing the quest is to embrace companionship. The quest is relational. Growth in the quest relies upon having wise teachers, caring relationships, a commitment to justice, sensitivity to the wonder of nature, embracing beauty, and creative responses to suffering.[13] Learning to sing a new song does not just come from the radio or worship or a downloaded playlist. Our lives discover how to sing a new song "born of all the new growth" that comes from being centered in our selves, centered in life itself, and centered in God.

We are carried on the quest by singing. Howard Thurman wrote about the ability of enslaved African Americans to create, through their spirituals, music that enabled them to resist having their value defined by their circumstances. He declares them to be among "the great religious thinkers of the human race. They made a worthless life, the life of chattel property, a mere thing, a body, *worth living!*"[14] What songs carry you through joyful and troubling times? The question is not asking, "can you carry a tune?" But, "do you have a tune that carries you?" Deep is the insatiable hunger to sing a new song!

*QUEST*ING WITH *QUEST*IONS

We usually think of a quest as the means to destinations. Even more important is to understand the quest *as the destination*. Being on the quest is to say yes to God's call upon one's life. Yes to feed the deep hunger. Yes to vocation. The "yes" is arrival to the destination. Thurman says, "It may be that seeking and finding, questing and finding, are one and the same thing."[15] To be on the quest is fulfillment even if we do not see another sunrise.

Thurman asserts that seeking is not only what humans do to address their deep hunger for God; seeking is what God does in response to God's deep hunger for us. He writes, "the God of religious experience is a seeking and a beseeching God."[16] Whether God seeking humanity or humanity seeking God, the quest is a holy activity that declares deep hunger for relationship.

The quest is a destination with difficult challenges that evoke never-ending questions: How do I discern what is correct among the myriad opportunities and decisions I face? Who and what have authority to inform and guide this journey? Should these authorities be questioned? Must I embrace ancestral beliefs? To what extent do I accept the perspectives that others have about me? Should God be questioned? To what extent is my true identity dependent on community or separation from community? How clear am I about the "yes" given to this quest? The questions continue throughout the whole quest. Perhaps even on our deathbeds.

When the questions seem overwhelming, we may find ourselves not reaching for an anchor in the current, but heading for known territory to seek a fortress that secures us from doubt, confusion, questions, and questing. In such a time, we are wise to remember that questions are vital to questing faithfully. The opposite of faith is not doubt; the opposite of faith is certainty. Questions are more than an admission of not knowing. Questions can be an expression of humility as we journey into the mysteries of life and the Mystery of God.

In his "Introduction" to Pablo Neruda's *Book of Questions*, William O'Daly writes that "our greatest act of faith" may be "living in a state of visionary surrender to the elemental questions, free of the quiet desperation of clinging too tightly to answers."[17] Questions create a space-in-time for reflection. A question causes us to ponder all that informs the reason for the question. And when we confront something more significant than a rhetorical question, a question can cause us to pause and consider and reconsider a response—perhaps for the rest of our lives. Questions deepen our spirits to address the deep hunger.

In his sermons and lectures, Howard Thurman invited readers to explore for themselves the personal and collective dimensions of matters related to his speaking. For example, in his sermon on "The Prodigal Son," Thurman begins with a prayer in which he asks seventeen questions. The sermon does not attempt to give answers to those questions. Instead, his sermon reflects upon the story of the prodigal son so that he and his listeners have a resource to continue engaging these essential questions about "the kinds of people we are."[18] The questions and the sermon are provisions for their quests.

The questions that conclude each chapter of this book also have the intention of providing readers a resource for ongoing reflections for their quests. Basically, the questions not only focus on seminal themes of chapters, they create a space-in-time for readers to conceive their own questions. This process entrusts us to employ our capacities in the search for truth. In addition, for those times when the questions seem embarrassingly simple or exceedingly complex and confusing, or verging on taking God to court to adjudicate unmerited suffering, or so outside the bounds of orthodoxy that we wonder if we are approaching forbidden fruit—for such times—perhaps the question mulling inside us is: "Do I trust God with all my questions?"

This question is integral to what I believe Thurman poses as the most fundamental question of the spiritual journey: "Do I trust God with my life?" Our answer to this question informs the moods and decisions of every step of the journey. Perhaps we never answer this question once and for all. Perhaps we answer it step-by-step, and decision-by-decision.

I have previously written about Thurman's conviction that trust in God is the basis for experiencing the joy of questing as God intended:

> Only God can provide the security and confidence to face [the new challenges of the future]. Without trust in God, we are left to our fears, prejudices, ambitions, weapons, and obsessions with certainty (even in our theological constructions). With trust in God, life can be lived with a freedom that is not canceled when we find ourselves with diverse people, diverse religious beliefs, or even the newness of oneself.[19]

Thurman's trust is not conditioned on God granting requested favors. Neither is God trusted because fervent prayers or doctrinal statements can manage God. Thurman insists that total surrender to God is the basis for trust in God. The surrender fulfills the deep and insatiable hunger. Nothing is more assuring for us than our lives being grounded in God. The surrender is not made in a spirit of sullen resignation. God is not held in reserve in case or until all my efforts fail. Crudely stated, God is not a spare tire for emergency situations. We quest faithfully and joyfully when we ardently surrender our lives to God—the God who welcomes our questions.

While many questions are asked in this chapter, I close with just one: *"Do I trust God with my life?"* All subsequent questions take their shape from our yes or no to this question. As each of us is anchored in the current, I hope we delight in looking around and seeing each other as companions who have embraced the quest, who are responding to the deep insatiable hunger, who continue to discover new songs to sing, and who experience the liberating power of questions. I am thankful that Howard Thurman is among us as a guide for the journey taken and the journey to come.

Postlude

A Perpetual State of Relative Completion

ELESA COMMERSE

Stay ready for the unexpected, including the end of life, because when you need to be ready you won't have time to get ready. You'll either be ready or you won't. Some of the simplest and most meaningful ways to do so are anchored in doing your best to live in a perpetual state of relative completion. This means that on a daily basis you take stock and act on the areas of your life affected by how you answer the questions: To whom do you need to say thank you, I love you, I'm sorry, I forgive you, please forgive me, how can I best love you, is there anything I can do for you?

When all is said and done and we come to the end of our lives, what else will really matter except that we loved well, that we forgave and sought forgiveness, that we offered thanks. That we realized we were more together than alone, that we made of our lives an offering of service to those around us. That we left the world better than we found it, we lived lightly on the land, in peace and friendship with one another, and we sought to understand. In the end what will your legacy be? May it be a legacy of peace and kindness. Namaste.[1]

Notes

Introduction

1. Howard Thurman, *Meditations of the Heart* (New York: Harper & Row, 1953), 16.

2. Thurman, *Meditations of the Heart*, 28.

3. Luther E. Smith, *Howard Thurman: The Mystic as Prophet* (Richmond, IN: Friends United Press, 1991), 39.

4. Smith, *Howard Thurman*, 39.

5. Walter E. Fluker, ed., *The Papers of Howard Washington Thurman*, vol. 1, *My People Need Me* (Columbia: University of South Carolina Press, 2009), xliii.

6. Fluker, *Papers*, 1:1.

7. Fluker, *Papers*, 1:2.

8. Fluker, *Papers*, 1:2.

9. Fluker, *Papers*, 1:lii.

10. Fluker, *Papers*, 1:liv.

11. Fluker, *Papers*, 1:liv, lxi.

12. To exemplify the vast terrain covered and the diversity of audiences engaged on his teaching circuit, I have included an abbreviated list of Thurman's addresses from 1926–1928: National Student Conference (Milwaukee, Wisconsin); Iowa State Teacher's College (Cedar Falls, Iowa); Conference on International, Economic-Industrial and Family Relations and Educational Methods (Hillsdale, Michigan); Joint meeting of the cabinets and commissions of the YMCA and YWCA (Champaign, Illinois); Inter-Racial Council and Liberal Club at Ohio State University (Columbus, Ohio); Minister's Conference of Hampton Institute (Hampton, Virginia). For more information, see "Howard Thurman Chronology" in Fluker, *Papers*, 1:xcvii–c.

13. Howard Thurman, *Inward Journey* (New York: Harper, 1961), 38.

14. *Backs against the Wall*, documentary film, directed by Martin Doblmeier, 2019.

15. Fluker, *Papers*, 1:117.

16. Fluker, *Papers*, 1:lxix.

17. Howard Thurman, *With Head and Heart: The Autobiography of Howard Thurman* (San Diego: Harcourt Brace Jovanovich, 1981), 83.

18. Quinton Hosford Dixie and Peter R. Eisenstadt, *Visions of a Better World: Howard Thurman's Pilgrimage to India and the Origins of African American Non-violence*, with a foreword by Walter E. Fluker (Boston: Beacon Press, 2011), 185.

19. Howard Thurman, *Jesus and the Disinherited* (Boston: Beacon Press, 1996), 15.

20. Luther E. Smith, "Howard Thurman," in *Christian Spirituality: The Classics*, ed. Arthur Holder (New York: Routledge, 2009), 342.

21. Thurman, *With Head and Heart*, 132, 134.

22. Howard Thurman, "Those Who Walked with God," in *The Living Wisdom of Howard Thurman: A Visionary of Our Time* (Louisville, CO: Sounds True, 2010), audio recording.

23. Thurman, *With Head and Heart*, 89.

24. Thurman, *With Head and Heart*, 90.

25. Smith, *Howard Thurman*, 9.

26. Smith, *Howard Thurman*, 10.

27. Howard Thurman, *Footprints of a Dream: The Story of the Church for the Fellowship of All Peoples* (New York: Harper & Brothers, 1959), 24.

28. Smith, *Howard Thurman*, 10.

29. Walter E. Fluker, ed., *The Papers of Howard Washington Thurman*, vol. 3, *The Bold Adventure* (Columbia: University of South Carolina Press, 2009), xxxvii, xlii.

30. "Great Preachers: These 12—and Others—Bring America Back to the Churches," *Life*, 6 April 1953, 126.

31. Walter E. Fluker, ed., *The Papers of Howard Washington Thurman*, vol. 4, *The Soundless Passion of a Single Mind* (Columbia: University of South Carolina Press, 2009), xxii.

32. Fluker, *Papers*, 4:xxiv–xxv.

33. Fluker, *Papers*, 4:xxv.

34. Fluker, *Papers*, 4:xxvi.

35. Deborah Cramer, *Great Waters: An Atlantic Passage* (New York: W. W. Norton, 2002), 102–3.

36. Thurman, *With Head and Heart*, 8.

37. Thurman, *With Head and Heart*, 109.

38. Thurman, *With Head and Heart*, 54, quoting Daisy Rinehart, "The Call of the Open Sea," *The Literary Digest* 31 (October 1905): 548.

39. In Rainer Maria Rilke's well-loved book *Letters to a Young Poet*, Rilke urges his apprentice to live and love the questions.

Chapter 1: Longing for Reunion
with a Man I Never Met

1. Howard Thurman, *Disciplines of the Spirit* (New York: Harper & Row, 1963; Richmond, IN: Friends United Press, 1977), quoted in Walter Earl Fluker and Catherine Tumber, eds., *A Strange Freedom: The Best of Howard Thurman on Religious Experience and Public Life* (Boston: Beacon Press, 1998), 184.

2. Zalman Schachter-Shalomi, "What I Found in the Chapel," in *My Neighbor's Faith: Stories of Interreligious Encounter, Growth, and Transformation*, ed. Jennifer Howe Peace, Or N. Rose, and Gregory Mobley (Maryknoll, NY: Orbis Books, 2013), 207–10.

3. Thurman, *Disciplines*, 27–28.

4. Thurman, *Disciplines*, 29.

5. Quoted in *Howard Thurman: The Mystic as Prophet* by Luther E. Smith Jr. (Richmond, IN: Friends United Press, 1991 edition), 174–75.

6. Howard Thurman, *Footprints of a Dream: The Story of the Church for the Fellowship of All Peoples* (New York: Harper & Brothers, 1959), 16.

7. Quoted in Smith, *Howard Thurman*, 47.

8. Howard Thurman, *Jesus and the Disinherited* (Boston: Beacon Press, 1996), 18.

9. Smith, *Howard Thurman*, 71.

10. Thurman, *Footprints of a Dream*, 24.

Chapter 2: Listening for the Voice of Vocation

1. Milford Q. Sibley, "Quaker Mysticism: Its Context and Implications." https://universalistfriends.org/quf2000a.html.

2. Stephen W. Angell, "Howard Thurman and Quakers," *Quaker Theology* 16 (Fall-Winter 2009), http://tinyurl.com/jdtyuah.

3. Howard Thurman, *Mysticism and the Experience of Love*, Pendle Hill Pamphlet no. 115 (Wallingford, PA: Pendle Hill, 1961), 3.

4. Based on excerpts from Howard Thurman's baccalaureate address at Spelman College, May 4, 1980, as edited by Jo Moore Stewart for *The Spelman Messenger* 96, no. 4 (Summer 1980): 14–15.

5. This seems to be a gloss on Matthew 26:24: "The Son of Man will go just as it is written about him. But woe to that man who betrays the Son of Man! It would be better for him if he had not been born" (NIV).

6. Luther Smith, *Howard Thurman: Essential Writings* (Maryknoll, NY: Orbis Books, 2008), 57.

7. For more detail on the conduct of a Quaker Clearness Committee, see Parker J. Palmer, *A Hidden Wholeness: The Journey toward an Undivided Life* (San Francisco: Jossey-Bass, 2009), 129–50.

8. Smith, *Howard Thurman*, 30.

9. Pete Holloran, "Howard Thurman, 1899–1981," Found SF—San Francisco's Digital Archive, http://tinyurl.com/hpsm6mv.

10. Rainer Maria Rilke, *Letters to a Young Poet*, trans. M. D. Herter (New York: Norton, 1993), 35.

Interlude: The Gift of Good Counsel

1. Lerone Bennett Jr., "Howard Thurman: 20th Century Holy Man," *Ebony* 33, no. 4 (February 1978): 68.

Chapter 3: The Inward Sea

1. Howard Thurman, *Meditations of the Heart* (New York: Harper & Row, 1953), 16.

2. From Howard Thurman to Walter E. Fluker, 11 September 1979.

3. The allusion to the Angel with the Flaming Sword is a symbol used by Quaker George Fox, who describes his enlightening experience of union in this manner: "Now I was come up in the spirit through the Flaming Sword, into the Paradise of God. All things were new; and all the creation gave unto me another smell than before, beyond what words can utter. I knew nothing but pureness, and innocency, and righteousness; being renewed into the image of God by Christ Jesus, to the state of Adam, which he was in before he fell. The creation was opened to me, and it was showed me how all things had their names given them according to their nature and virtue." George Fox, *Journal of George Fox: Being an Historical Account of the Life, Travels* (Richmond, IN: Friends United Press; reprinted from 1908 edition), 97.

Thurman identifies "the Angel with the Flaming Sword" as a symbol of the price exacted for the transition from innocence to goodness—a sense of integrity, harmony, and wholeness. The Angel is set before the altar (Eden) to ensure that only those who exercise their inner authority and integrity can return to the garden (the *archē*, the beginning); therefore entry is only permitted for the true in heart who are willing to be cut asunder and dismembered by the burning sword. The price exacted for knowledge of Presence, *in sum*, is a return to the beginning, to creation.

4. Mark 1:1–3 ESV.

5. Walter E. Fluker interview with Peter Eisenstadt, 14 April 2016. Portions of this interview are published in "The Wider Ministry," in *The Papers of Howard Washington Thurman*, vol. 5, *The Wider Ministry, January 1963–April 1981* (Columbia: University of South Carolina Press, 2019).

6. Howard Thurman, *The Luminous Darkness: A Personal Interpretation of the Anatomy of Segregation and the Ground of Hope* (repr., Richmond, IN: Friends United Press, 1989; originally published New York: Harper & Row, 1965), 113.

7. *The Inward Journey* can be read as the last of a trilogy of meditations that encompassed Thurman's sermons and writings over a span of twelve years, beginning with a sermon series titled "Men Who Walked with God," delivered at the Fellowship Church in 1949. This trilogy of meditations comprises *Deep Is the Hunger: Meditations for Apostles of Sensitiveness* (New York: Harper & Brothers, 1951); *Meditations of the Heart*; and *The Inward Journey* (Richmond, IN: Friends United Press, 1961). "The Inward Journey" was also offered as a series of nine sermons given from October to December 1961. After an introductory sermon, Thurman spoke on "The Mystic Will—Jacob Boehme," "Meister Eckhardt," "The Inner Light" (two sermons), "St. Francis," "Plotinus: The Inner Journey," and "St. Augustine: Architect of a New Faith" (two sermons). See introduction to volume 4 of Fluker, *Papers*.

8. Thurman, *The Inward Journey*, 96.

9. Walter Earl Fluker, *Ethical Leadership: The Quest for Character, Civility, and Community* (Minneapolis: Fortress Press, 2009), 65.

10. Howard Thurman, *The Creative Encounter: An Interpretation of Religion and the Social Witness* (New York: Harper & Row, 1954; Richmond, IN: Friends United Press, 1972), 20.

11. "Religious experience in its profoundest dimension is the finding of man [*sic*] by God and the finding of God by man [*sic*]." Thurman, *Creative Encounter*, 39.

12. Thurman, *Creative Encounter*, 33.

13. Thurman, *Creative Encounter*.

14. See Brian Drayton and William P. Taber Jr., *A Language for the Inner Landscape: Spiritual Wisdom from the Quaker Movement* (Philadelphia: Tract Association of Friends, 2015); and Douglas V. Steere, *On Beginning from Within, and On Listening to Another* (New York, Evanston, and London: Harper & Row, 1964).

15. See Howard Thurman, "Knowledge . . . Shall Vanish Away," in *The Inward Journey*, 96.

16. See Fluker, *Ethical Leadership*, chap. 7, "Remembering, Retelling, and Reliving Our Stories," 167–74.

17. See Walter Earl Fluker, *The Ground Has Shifted: The Future of the Black Church in Post-Racial America* (New York: New York University Press, 2016), 189. *Le point le verge* is an apex, or still point, the "center of our nothingness where one meets God—and is found completely in His mercy." See Albert J. Raboteau's quotation of Thomas Merton, *Conjectures of a Guilty Bystander* (New York: Crown Publishing Group, 2009), 127, 148, 155.

18. Thurman, *The Inward Journey*, 40, 65.

19. Howard Thurman, "Who Are You?," meditation from We Believe series, Boston Public Radio, http://archives.bu.edu/web/howard-thurman/virtual-listening-room/detail?id=350015.

20. Thurman, "Who Are You?"

21. Thurman, "A Strange Freedom," in *The Inward Journey*, 37–38.

22. See Thurman's discussion on commitment in Howard Thurman, *Disciplines of the Spirit* (New York: Harper & Row, 1963; Richmond, IN: Friends United Press, 1977), 13–37.

23. See my discussion of Thurman's ministry to Martin Luther King Jr. in Harlem Hospital in October 1958 in *Ethical Leadership*, 28–32.

24. Thurman, *Disciplines,* 19.

25. Thurman, *Disciplines,* 34.

26. Howard Thurman, *The Search for Common Ground: An Inquiry into the Basis of Man's Experience of Community* (Richmond, IN: Friends United Press, 2000), 31–32.

27. Howard Thurman, "The Third Component," Oct. 26, 1958, http://archives.bu.edu/web/howard-thurman/virtual-listening-room/detail?id=340585. Thurman discusses the "third component," or the relationship between two or more entities that is already given and must be discovered or realized. He elaborates with examples of different interactions he has witnessed between people and nature.

28. Howard Thurman, "We Believe" television series, 25 September 1959, Thurman Papers, Boston University, p. 91.

29. James Baldwin, *The Fire Next Time* (New York: Penguin Books, 1993), 98.

30. Howard Thurman, "A Strange Freedom," in Walter E. Fluker and Catherine Tumber, eds., *A Strange Freedom: The Best of Howard Thurman on Religious Experience and Public Life* (Boston: Beacon Press, 1998), 37–38.

31. Thurman, "A Strange Freedom," in *The Inward Journey*, 1; see also "America in Search of a Soul," the Robbins Lecture Series, University of Redlands, Redlands, CA (20 January 1976), Thurman Papers, Boston University, 9.

32. Thurman, "America in Search," 10.

33. Thurman, "America in Search," 10.

34. "Freedom under God," Washington University, Second Century Convocation (February 1955), Thurman Papers, Boston University, p. 2.

35. See Luther Smith's "Community: Partnership of Freedom and Responsibility," in Henry J. Young, ed., *God and Human Freedom: A Festschrift in Honor of Howard Thurman* (Richmond, IN: Friends United Press, 1983), 23–31. Here Smith indicates that responsibility in Thurman means both "response-ability" and "accountability."

36. Thurman says, "The moment I transfer responsibility for my own actions, I relinquish my own free initiative. I become an instrument in another's hands. This is the iniquity of all forms of human slavery. The slave is not a responsible person and the result of slavery is the destruction, finally, of any sense of alternatives." Thurman, "Freedom under God," 2.

37. Thurman, "Man and the Experience of Freedom," California State College, Long Beach, California, March 19, 1969, Thurman Papers, Special Collections, Mugar Memorial Library, Boston University, 5.

38. Howard Thurman, "The Freedom of the Human Spirit," Carmel Valley Manor, January 24, 1971, Thurman Papers, Howard Gotlieb Archival Research Center, Boston University.

39. Howard Thurman, "Freedom under God," 3. Howard Gotlieb Archival Research Center, Boston University.

40. Thurman, "Freedom under God," 3.

41. Thurman, "Freedom under God," 3; see also, Thurman, "America in Search of a Soul," in Walter Earl Fluker and Catherine Tumber, *A Strange Freedom*, 265–72.

42. Thurman, "Freedom under God," 27.

43. Howard Thurman, I. Hester Lectureship, "The Dilemma of the Religious Professional," delivered at Golden Gate Baptist Theological Seminary, Mill Valley, CA, February 8–12, 1971.

44. Howard Thurman, Pendle Hill Pamphlet no. 115 (Wallingford, PA: Pendle Hill, 1961), 5.

45. Thurman, *The Inward Journey*, 121.

Chapter 4: Thurman-eutics

1. Howard Thurman, *The Creative Encounter: An Interpretation of Religion and the Social Witness* (New York: Harper & Row, 1954; Richmond, IN: Friends United Press, 1972), 36–37.

2. Howard Thurman, *Deep Is the Hunger: Meditations for Apostles of Sensitiveness* (Richmond, IN: Friends United Press, 2000), 64. The additions of feminine pronouns are my own. Thurman wrote in an era where the patriarchal nature of language was not yet widely acknowledged. I believe if Thurman were alive now, he would be mindful of including the whole spectrum of gender and sexual diversity. In any case, as a cis-woman who has read and journeyed in her life with Thurman's writings and teachings, I have always read his "male" designations as including all genders. My small revisions to his quotations included in this chapter make that explicit, with hopes that he is accessible to others who struggle to see their pronouns and identities present in Thurman's thinking; in my study of him, we are wholly included, considered, and valued.

3. This uses the phrase "head and heart," which often presupposes Thurman's life and thoughts as communicated in his autobiography: *With Head and Heart: The Autobiography of Howard Thurman*, 1st Harvest/HBJ ed. (San Diego: Harcourt Brace Jovanovich, 1981).

4. Howard Thurman, *Meditations of the Heart* (Boston: Beacon Press, 1999 [1953]), 36–37; excerpted in Howard Thurman and Luther E. Smith Jr., *Howard Thurman: Essential Writings*, Modern Spiritual Masters Series (Maryknoll, NY: Orbis Books, 2006), 172–73.

5. Thurman, *The Creative Encounter*, 23–24.

6. The study of hermeneutics is the study of how humans make meaning of the world, interpreting the images and words we encounter along the way. Sometimes we are conscious of this meaning-making process; but most often, we are not. Consequently, hermeneutics is the human endeavor to heighten our awareness of how we interpret our world and texts. As a subject of academic study in theology and philosophy, hermeneutics is an attempt to articulate how we come to understand something as meaningful and as such, it is fundamentally a descriptive task. It seeks to explain, "How do you know something has meaning and how do you arrive at an understanding of its significance?"

7. Thurman, *Deep Is the Hunger*, 145–46.

8. Thurman, *The Creative Encounter*, 20–21; also see, Thurman and Smith, *Howard Thurman: Essential Writings*, 37.

9. Thurman, *The Creative Encounter*, 27.

10. Howard Thurman, *Temptations of Jesus: Five Sermons* (Richmond, IN: Friends United Press, 1978), 14–15.

11. Howard Thurman, "If I Knew You," in *Meditations of the Heart*, 115–16.

12. Howard Thurman, *Jesus and the Disinherited* (Boston: Beacon Press, 1996), 5.

13. Thurman, *Jesus and the Disinherited*, 5.

14. Thurman, *Jesus and the Disinherited*, 23.

15. Thurman, *Jesus and the Disinherited*, 36.

16. Thurman, *Jesus and the Disinherited*, 24.

17. Thurman, *Jesus and the Disinherited*, 23–24.

18. Thurman, *Jesus and the Disinherited*, xi, x.

19. Thurman, *Jesus and the Disinherited*, viii.

Chapter 5: Prophetic Service and Global Change

1. Howard Thurman, *Meditations of the Heart* (Boston: Beacon Press, 1981), 147–49.

2. Walter E. Fluker and Catherine Tumber, eds., *A Strange Freedom: The Best of Howard Thurman on Religious Experience and Public Life* (Boston: Beacon Press, 1998), 3.

3. Fluker and Tumber, *Strange Freedom*, 3.

4. Marian Wright Edelman, *Guide My Feet: Prayers and Meditations on Loving and Working for Children* (Boston: Beacon Press, 1995), xiv.

5. Howard Thurman, *Jesus and the Disinherited* (Boston: Beacon Press, 1996).

6. Thurman, *Jesus and the Disinherited*, 23.

7. Luther E. Smith Jr., *Howard Thurman: The Mystic as Prophet* (Richmond, IN: Friends United Press, 2007), 19–20.

8. Smith, *Howard Thurman*, 19–20.

9. Marian Wright Edelman, *Lanterns: A Memoir of Mentors* (Boston: Beacon Press, 1999), 3, 8.

10. Howard Thurman, *The Centering Moment* (New York: Harper & Row, 1969), 20. Emphasis mine.

11. Howard Thurman, *The Inward Journey* (Richmond, IN: Friends United Press, 2007), 109.

12. Thurman, *The Inward Journey*, 110.

13. Edelman, *Lanterns*, xiii.

14. Theodore Roosevelt, "Citizenship in a Republic" (speech, Sorbonne, Paris, April 23, 1910), https://assets.aspeninstitute.org/content/uploads/files/content/upload/Action%20Forum%202013%20-%20Reading%20Packet%20-%20July%2031.pdf.

15. Edelman, *Lanterns*, 109.

16. Reinhold Niebuhr, *The Irony of American History* (Chicago: The University of Chicago Press, 2010), 62.

17. Amelia Boynton Robinson, www.ameliaboyntonrobinson.org/.

18. Thurman, *Meditations of the Heart*, 149.

19. Thurman, *The Inward Journey*, 64–65.

Chapter 6: Where Freedom Forms

1. Howard Thurman, "Mysticism and Social Change" (lecture 4, Eden Theological Seminary, St. Louis, MO, February 16, 1939).

2. Edward R. Berchick, Jessica C. Barnett, and Rachel D. Upton, "Health Insurance Coverage in the United States: 2018," U.S. Department of Commerce, November 2019, census.gov.

3. Walter Earl Fluker et al., eds., *The Papers of Howard Washington Thurman*, vol. 2, *Christian, Who Calls Me Christian? April 1936–August 1943* (Columbia: University of South Carolina Press, 2009-2019), 190.

4. Fluker, *Papers*, 2:213.

5. Walter E. Fluker and Catherine Tumber, *A Strange Freedom: The Best of Howard Thurman on Religious Experience and Public Life* (Boston: Beacon Press, 1998), 120.

6. Eric Klinenberg, *Palaces for the People: How Social Infrastructure Can Help Fight Inequality, Polarization, and the Decline of Civic Life* (New York: Crown Publishing Group, 2018), 5.

7. Patrisse Khan-Cullors and Asha Bandele, *When They Call You A Terrorist: A Black Lives Matter Memoir* (New York: St. Martin's Press, 2018), 216.

8. Thurman, "Mysticism and Social Change."

9. Thurman, *A Strange Freedom*, 120.

Chapter 7: Mysticism and Social Action

1. Howard Thurman, "Religion in a Time of Crisis," *The Garrett Tower* 18, no. 4 (August 1943): 3.

2. Howard Thurman, *The Luminous Darkness* (Richmond, IN: Friends United Press, 1989), x.

3. Thurman, *Luminous Darkness*, 59.

4. Cofounded by Howard Thurman and Dr. Alfred Fisk in San Francisco in 1944, the Church for the Fellowship of All Peoples (aka Fellowship Church) was the first intentionally interracial, intercultural church—in both congregation and leadership—in the United States.

5. Arleigh Prelow, InSpirit Communication and Film, *Howard Thurman: Spirit of a Movement*, documentary short commissioned by the Museum of the African Diaspora, San Francisco, CA, 2005.

6. Howard Thurman, *Mysticism and the Experience of Love* (Wallingford, PA: Pendle Hill Publications, 1961), 6.

7. Howard Thurman, "Mysticism and Social Change" (1939), in *A Strange Freedom*, Walter E. Fluker and Catherine Tumber, eds. (Boston: Beacon Press, 1998), 116.

8. Thurman, *Strange Freedom*, 121.

9. Not everyone responds to the mystic encounter with a sense of social commitment, but this is descriptive of Thurman's brand of affirmation mysticism.

10. Eugene V. Debs, Statement to the Court, upon Being Convicted of Violating the Sedition Act, September 18, 1918, transcribed by John W. Metz, https://www.marxists.org/archive/debs/works/1918/court.htm.

11. Abraham Joshua Heschel, *Moral Grandeur and Spiritual Audacity: Essays Edited by Susannah Heschel* (New York: Farrar, Straus and Giroux, 1996), 399.

12. Luther Smith, *Howard Thurman: The Mystic as Prophet* (Richmond, IN: Friends United Press, 1992), 208.

13. Howard Thurman, "Mysticism and Social Action," Lawrence Lecture on Religion and Society, First Unitarian Church of Berkeley (Kensington, CA, October 13, 1978).

14. Thurman, "Mysticism and Social Action."

15. Prelow, *Howard Thurman*.

16. Michael Bernard Beckwith, "Pain Pushes until the Vision Pulls," https://www.aol.com/video/view/dr-michael-bernard-beckwith-pain-pushes-until-the-vision-pulls/57f80fa61c689930eeb0fe49/.

17. For more see: Sustaining the Soul of Activism, https://onelifeinstitute.org/sustaining-activism.

18. The term "kin-dom" was introduced by Ada María Isasi-Díaz in *Mujerista Theology* (Maryknoll, NY: Orbis Books, 1996), 89.

19. "A Tribute to Life," in *The Living Wisdom of Howard Thurman* audio collection, Sounds True, 2010.

20. Howard Thurman, *With Head and Heart* (New York: Harcourt, Brace & Company, 1979), 269.

Chapter 8: "The Growing Edge" of Life and Ministry

1. Howard Thurman, *The Growing Edge* (Richmond, IN: Friends United Press, 1956), epigraph.

2. Howard Thurman, *With Head and Heart: The Autobiography of Howard Thurman* (New York: Harcourt Brace & Company, 1979), 3–4.

3. Thurman, *With Head and Heart*, 4.

4. Thurman, *With Head and Heart*, 4.

5. See dedication page of Thurman, *With Head and Heart*.

6. Thurman, *With Head and Heart*, 73.

7. Thurman, *With Head and Heart*, 83.

8. Howard Thurman, "The Growing Edge," sermon, in *The Growing Edge*, 177.

9. See Howard Thurman, *Deep River and the Negro Spiritual Speaks of Life and Death* (Richmond, IN: Friends United Press, 1975), and Luke A. Powery, *Dem Dry Bones: Preaching, Death, and Hope* (Minneapolis: Fortress Press, 2012).

10. Pauli Murray, *Dark Testament and Other Poems* (Norwalk, CT: Silvermine, 1970), 22.

11. Thurman, *With Head and Heart*, 17.

12. Craig Detweiler, *iGods: How Technology Shapes Our Spiritual and Social Lives* (Grand Rapids: Brazos Press, 2013).

13. Thurman, *With Head and Heart*, 144.

14. This story can be found at http://news.bbc.co.uk/2/hi/africa/662472 .stm.

Chapter 9: In Search of Thurman's Apostles

1. Howard Thurman, *Footprints of a Dream: The Story of the Church for the Fellowship of All Peoples* (New York: Harper, 1959), 11.

2. Walter Earl Fluker et al., eds., *The Papers of Howard Washington Thurman*, vol. 3, *The Bold Adventure, September 1943–May 1949* (Columbia: University of South Carolina Press, 2015), xxii–xxiii.

3. Fluker, *The Papers of Howard Washington Thurman*, 3:xxiii–xxiv. Fluker notes a divide in the African American community in San Francisco. Those who lived there before the drastic rise in African American residents (before 1940) were prejudiced against those who migrated in during the growth. In addition, Fluker highlights Thurman's disgust at the apathy of American Christianity toward race issues, in particular segregation. See also Albert S. Broussard, *Black San Francisco: The Struggle for Racial Equality in the West, 1900–1954* (Lawrence: University Press of Kansas, 1993), 143–65.

4. *CBS News,* https://www.cbsnews.com/news/children-at-border-facility -children-living-inhumane-conditions-texas-border-facility-doctors-attorneys

-say/; *Fox 13 News*, http://www.fox13news.com/news/immigration-holding
-facility-061818; Maria Sacchetti, *The Washington Post*, https://www
.washingtonpost.com/immigration/kids-in-cages-house-hearing-to-examine
-immigration-detention-as-democrats-push-for-more-information/2019/07/10
/3cc53006-a28f-11e9-b732-41a79c2551bf_story.html?noredirect=on&utm
_term=.c32f7616b73e

5. Michelle Alexander, *The New Jim Crow: Mass Incarceration in the Age of Colorblindness* (New York: The New Press, 2010); Ta-Nehisi Coates, *Between the World and Me* (New York: Spiegal & Grau, 2015); Carol Anderson, *White Rage: The Unspoken Truth of Our Racial Divide* (New York: Bloomsbury USA, 2016).

6. I chose seven years because seven years ago Trayvon Martin (seventeen-year-old African American boy) was shot and killed in Sanford, Florida, by George Zimmerman—a neighborhood watch captain. Zimmerman claimed that Martin looked suspicious and called 911. The 911 operator told Zimmerman to stand down; instead, Zimmerman engages Martin and, in the struggle, kills him. The nation went into an uproar. The president at that time—President Barack Obama—said that the nation was in need of soul searching. Zimmerman was found not guilty, and many protests ensued. After the killing of Martin, many more high-profile murders of unarmed African Americans took place: George Floyd, Breanna Taylor, Sandra Bland, Tamir Rice, Philando Castile, Freddie Gray, Eric Garner, Michael Brown, Rekia Boyd, Alton Sterling, and Charleena Lyles. There were plenty of killings before Martin, namely, among others, Oscar Grant and Amadou Diallo. Martin's case caught the national spotlight in such a way that those after him got high levels of national attention.

7. Thurman, journal entry July 15, 1944, in Fluker, *The Papers of Howard Washington Thurman*, 3:87. Emphasis mine. Fluker notes that the actual date was probably July 16, 1944, because Thurman said that the day of the entry was Sunday. Obviously, Thurman wrote the entry after July 16 because he records what happened on July 23 and July 30 in that same entry.

8. Howard Thurman, "The Cultural and Spiritual Prospect for a Nation Emerging from Total War," in Fluker, *The Papers of Howard Washington Thurman*, 3:104–8. Thurman "delivered [this speech] in the waning months of World War II" in 1945.

9. Fluker, *The Papers of Howard Washington Thurman*, 3:106.

10. Howard Thurman, "Apostles of Sensitiveness," in Fluker, *The Papers of Howard Washington Thurman*, 3:170–74. Thurman preached this sermon at the Cathedral of St. John the Divine on February 10, 1946, in New York City.

11. Thurman, "Apostles of Sensitiveness," 171.

12. Thurman, "Apostles of Sensitiveness," 172.

13. Thurman, "Apostles of Sensitiveness," 172.

14. Thurman, "Apostles of Sensitiveness," 173.

15. Fluker, *The Papers of Howard Washington Thurman*, 3:108.

16. Fluker, *The Papers of Howard Washington Thurman*, 3:107.

17. Fluker, *The Papers of Howard Washington Thurman*, 3:173.

18. Howard Thurman, *The Search for Common Ground: An Inquiry into the Basis of Man's Experience of Community* (Richmond, IN: Friends United Press, 2000), 80.

19. Marianne Williamson, "Our Deepest Fear," in *A Return to Love: Reflections on the Principles of "A Course in Miracles"* (New York: Harper Collins Publishing, 1992), 190–91.

20. Howard Thurman, *Deep Is the Hunger: Meditations for Apostles of Sensitiveness* (Richmond, IN: Friends United Press, 2000), 41.

21. Thurman, *Deep Is the Hunger*, 42.

22. Thurman, *Deep Is the Hunger*, 43.

23. Thurman, *Deep Is the Hunger*, 160–61.

Chapter 10: When the Magic Happens I Struggle to Catch My Breath

1. Howard Thurman, *Meditations of the Heart* (New York: Harper & Row, 1953), 125–26.

2. Howard Thurman, "Those Who Walked with God," in *The Living Wisdom of Howard Thurman: A Visionary of Our Time* (Louisville, CO: Sounds True, 2010), audio recording.

Conclusion

1. To hear a section of this sermon, please listen to "A Tribute to Life" in the six-compact disc recording of Thurman's sermons, meditations, and lectures titled *The Living Wisdom of Howard Thurman: A Visionary for Our Time*, edited by Vincent Harding, Liza Rankow, Luther E. Smith Jr., and Olive Thurman Wong (Boulder, CO: Sounds True, 2010). The recording was played at Thurman's memorial service.

2. Rufus Jones became a seminal mentor to Thurman. See Luther E. Smith Jr., *Howard Thurman: The Mystic as Prophet* (Washington, DC: University Press of America, 1981; Richmond, IN; Friends United Press, 2007), 33–38.

3. Smith, *Howard Thurman*, 21–44.

4. See Luke 11:9–13 as the Scripture that speaks to the necessity of seeking as an essential act of faith. Thurman's determination to pursue religious insight through seeking is in his book *The Search for Common Ground: An Inquiry into the Basis of Man's Experience of Community* (New York: Harper & Row, 1971; Richmond, IN: Friends United Press, 1986).

5. Thurman, "The Quest of the Human Spirit."

6. Howard Thurman, *Deep River: Reflections on the Religious Insight of Certain of the Negro Spirituals* (New York: Harper & Row, 1955; Richmond, IN: Friends United Press, 1975), 13.

7. Thurman, *Deep River*, 77.

8. Thurman, "The Quest of the Human Spirit."

9. Halcyon Backhouse, ed., *The Best of Meister Eckhart* (New York: Crossroad Publishing, 1993), 33–34. Also see pages 88, 132–34, and 141. Thurman references Meister Eckhart on this assertion in his *Disciplines of the Spirit* (New York: Harper & Row, 1963; Richmond, IN: Friends United Press, 1977), 16–17.

10. Howard Thurman, *The Creative Encounter: An Interpretation of Religion and the Social Witness* (New York: Harper & Row, 1954; Richmond, IN: Friends United Press, 1972), 40.

11. Howard Thurman, *Deep Is the Hunger* (Richmond, IN: Friends United Press, 2000), 69.

12. Rabindranath Tagore, trans., *Songs of Kabir* (New York: The Macmillan Company, 1915), 28.

13. See Thurman, *Disciplines* (64–85), for Thurman's understanding of suffering as a discipline that is a consequence of freedom and the willingness to experience pain in order to be faithful to one's commitment.

14. Howard Thurman, *The Negro Spiritual Speaks of Life and Death* (New York: Harper & Row, 1947). Reprinted by Friends United Press in 1975 as a single volume with *Deep River*. The quote is from this single volume, page 135.

15. Thurman, "The Quest of the Human Spirit."

16. Thurman, *The Creative Encounter*, 38.

17. Pablo Neruda, *The Book of Questions*, translated with introduction by William O'Daly (Port Townsend, WA: Copper Canyon Press, 2001), x.

18. See Howard Thurman, *Sermons on the Parables*, edited with an introduction by David B. Gowler and Kipton E. Jensen (Maryknoll, NY: Orbis Books, 2018), 26–36.

19. Luther E. Smith Jr., introduction to *Howard Thurman: Essential Writings*, by Howard Thurman (Maryknoll, NY: Orbis Books, 2006), 32.

Postlude

1. Elesa Commerse, "The Lightning Rod of Loss and How It Compels Us to Be Kind," *Yoga Chicago* (March/April 2020), https://yogachicago.com/2020/02/the-lightning-rod-of-loss-and-how-it-compels-us-to-be-kind/.

Index

CPSIA information can be obtained
at www.ICGtesting.com
Printed in the USA
FSHW020227251020
75094FS